**Land.
Milk.
Honey.**

Written and edited by
Rachel Gottesman, Tamar Novick, Iddo Ginat, Dan Hasson, Yonatan Cohen

Text editing and translation
English: **Daria Kassovsky**
Hebrew: **Daphna Raz**
Arabic: **Raji Bathish** (translation), **Dr. Basilius Bawardi** (editing)

Graphic design
Dana Gez, Studio Gimel2

Graphic design assistants
Ella Yehudai, Noam Maoz, Michal Zur

Copyright management
Shira Yasur, Bar Mussan Levi

Printing and binding
AR Printing Ltd., Tel Aviv

ISBN 978-3-03860-247-7

© 2021, the editors; Nine Lives Press, Jerusalem; Park Books AG, Zurich

© texts: the editors and authors, unless indicated otherwise

© photographs: courtesy of the exhibiting photographers

© Archival photos and images: see image credits

Distribution in Israel
Nine Lives Press
24 Gordon St., Tel Aviv
uriel@9livespress.com
www.9livespress.com

Distribution in the rest of the world
Park Books
Niederdorfstrasse 54
8001 Zurich
Switzerland
www.park-books.com

Park Books is being supported by the Federal Office of Culture with a general subsidy for the years 2021–2024.

All rights reserved; no part of this publication may be reproduced, stored in a retrieval system or transmitted in any form or by any means, electronic, mechanical, photocopying, recording, or otherwise, without the prior written consent of the publisher.

Every effort has been made to locate the copyright holders of the textual, visual, and other materials used in this book and the source of each photograph reproduced in it. Should there be any errors or omissions, we apologize and shall be pleased to make acknowledgments in future editions.

Land.
Milk.
Honey.

Animal Stories in Imagined Landscapes

Rachel Gottesman
Tamar Novick
Iddo Ginat
Dan Hasson
Yonatan Cohen

PARK BOOKS

תשע נשמות

The Israeli Pavilion
The 17th International Architecture Exhibition
La Biennale di Venezia

Land. Milk. Honey.
Animal Stories in Imagined Landscapes

Curators
Dan Hasson
Iddo Ginat
Rachel Gottesman
Yonatan Cohen
Tamar Novick

Curatorial advisor
Yael Messer

Advisory and scientific support
The Steinhardt Museum of Natural History, Israel National Center for Biodiversity Studies, Tel Aviv University

Participating artists
Shadi Habib Allah, Netta Laufer, Apollo Legisamo, Daniel Meir

Photographers
Aviad Bar Ness, Sarale Gur Lavi, Adam Havkin, Netta Laufer, Eran Levin, Gili Merin

Research assistants
Bar Mussan Levi, Omri Levy, Tamar Ofer, Idan Sidi, Maya Dann, Michael Cidor

Graphic design
Dana Gez, Studio Gimel2

Commissioner & producer
Michael Gov, Productions Den Ltd., Tel Aviv

Pavilion commissioner & manager
Arad Turgeman

Assistant producer
Shira Yasur

Exhibition construction
Team Festo Israel; Shaul Ben Or, Palbam; Shai Dekel, Sergei Sonin

Video editing
Doron Levene

Exhibition installation
Techwood s.a.s. di Salvato Niccolò & c.

Original concept
based on Tamar Novick's
doctoral dissertation, 2014

Contents

021 Creatures in Council
025 Introduction

-
Chapter 1
Land
034 Geography
060 Holy Land
074 Taxonomies
088 Erotic Soil
092 Portraying Progress
100 Lamentation

-
Chapter 2
Milk and Honey
117 The Making of the Hebrew Cow
187 Bee Colonization
219 Scapegoat

-
Chapter 3
High Waters
260 The Water Buffalo
272 The Swamp
298 Fauna & Flora of Huleh
306 Settlers
310 The Draining Project
348 Last Thoughts on Plenitude

-
Epilogue
353 Bunker

382 Bibliography
385 Index of Images and Sources
388 Acknowledgments

Creatures in Council.

Inspired by a Palestinian fable documented by Philip J. Baldensperger

After God created the world and all the living creatures in it, He assembled all of them, gave each animal its territory and determined its foods, concluding with man: "Be fruitful, and multiply, and replenish the earth, and subdue it: and have dominion over the fish of the sea, and over the fowl of the air, and over every living thing that moveth upon the earth." This was the first animal council. The second animal council was convened by Noah on the eve of the flood: he summoned all the animals and put them, two by two, into the ark. Centuries and millennia passed, and the day came when the animals could no longer bear their condition and decided to discuss man's attitude towards them and the great harm inflicted on them by humans. This was the third animal council.

The fox served as secretary. For years he gathered evidence and documents, and it was time to make them public. The gathering place, the fox decreed, would be Lake Huleh, where the animals would enjoy a safe haven and abundant food of all kinds. There, the gathering would also be hidden from human interference, as people rarely reach the deep parts of the swamp and never spend the night there. It was therefore agreed upon, and the date and hour were set.

On the appointed day, the animals arrived at the meeting place hidden at the heart of the swamp. They passed through the thicket of papyrus—such a thick, floating wood that nothing could be seen through it except green

Sarale Gur Lavi, Natural History Museum Collections, 2020 (the Steinhardt Museum of Natural History, Tel Aviv University) »

reeds rising high up, and one cannot tell whether one's foot was treading on solid ground or water, or whether it is another material altogether, neither solid nor liquid, but in-between, neither hard nor soft. The heat was great and stupefying, and once they crossed the dense thicket, the beasts found themselves on the edge of a clear pool. Water lilies and nymphaea floated on the surface, which reflected the azure sky. The place was perfect for one and all; it boasted plenty of fresh water and food for all species, varieties, and families: plants for the herbivores, deer and fallow deer for the carnivores, fish en masse for the waterfowl, rodents for the birds of prey.

The animals awaited nightfall; it was a full moon night and no man was to be seen. Quietly, they gathered round. The lion king, who came all the way from the Euphrates River, sat in the middle, his mane blowing in the wind. The birds, large and small, perched on the tree branches. Fish, turtles, frogs, and toads stuck their heads out of the pool water. The wild animals gathered on one side of the pool: mice and bats, the brown bear of Mt. Hermon, the leopard and the striped, hungry-looking hyena, the lone wolf, the cheetah, the jackal, the wild cat, the boar, as well as the otter, porcupine, hedgehog, mole, rat, mongoose, gazelle, badger, and snake. The farm animals gathered on the other side: a broad-breasted bull and a Billy-goat, sheep, a camel and a donkey, a horse and a mule, a rooster and a water buffalo. The dog and cat came last.

The carnivores spoke on the first night. The bear said: "Humans shut themselves in their stone houses"; and the lion said: "They will not let us hunt them down and devour them"; and the leopard added: "They have broken the world order."

The herbivores spoke on the second night. The ram said: "Humans chase us"; and the monkey said: "We, who have lived in this land long before them, are now forced to seek refuge"; and the gazelle said: "They hunt us with bow and arrow, and rifle"; and the wild boar added: "They are destroying the swamps and streams that were our home"; and the fruit bat concluded: "They poison our food."

On the third night, the farm animals spoke. The sheep said: "The sons and daughters of man bully us"; and the donkey said: "They lock us up behind fences"; and the goat added: "They take the milk intended for our young"; and the horse said: "They beat us"; and the cow added: "They leave us to lie in filth." At last the dog spoke: "I love Adam's sons and daughters. They let me sleep at their feet and pet me."

On the fourth night the songbirds, birds of prey, and waterfowl spoke—the stork, heron, egret, duck, pelican, and the great eagle. On the fifth night, the fish, the frogs, and the snails spoke, and on the sixth—the arthropod reptiles and worms.

On the seventh night of the gathering, there was no animal left to speak. Silence fell on the swamp and everyone watched the moon's waning crescent reflected in the water, flickering. Toward the end of the night, the papyrus murmurs were heard across the water: "We are one. We sprouted from the same seed, from the same breath of God; we are all brethren in the Tree of Life; an invisible web connects us all—land, animals, and plants. It penetrates the bowels of the earth, and its roots lie far back in the distant past, at the beginning of time."

After all of this the animals drew close together to form a tight circle. The bear stood beside the gazelle, the fox next to the house mouse, a stork and a heron by the fish and toads. And as if given a sign from heaven, they all began to growl, whistle and creak, first softly and then louder and louder, until a great roar came from out of the papyrus thicket, and an ancient breeze rose from the swamp and blew in the world: it blew over the water lilies and nymphaea; on the reed huts of the Bedouin tribe of Areb al Ghawarina; it blew into the stone houses and fortified cities of man's sons and daughters, and knocked down stone walls and iron gates. Then the sun rose, and the council dispersed.

Humans awakened from their sleep as the earth shook at dawn, only to learn that their tongues were lost and they had no language or memory or stories to tell. They reverted to being field animals like any other, bereft of their supremacy. Struck by terrible hunger, they went out of their homes to search for food, just as the animals.

Introduction.

An ancient fable tells how the entire animal kingdom gathered near Lake Huleh and discussed their grave situation: man was hunting them down, destroying their habitats, and enslaving them.

The animals of that forgotten council are the protagonists of this book; a variety of mammals, insects, and birds—bears, stags, bats, pelicans, bees, cows, goats, etc. Their stories unfold a spatial history of a place from a zoocentric perspective. The place is the "land flowing with milk and honey"—the geographic extent stretching between the Jordan River and the Mediterranean Sea; a land which many consider "holy" and "promised"; a much contested territory which is the political entity of both Palestine and Israel.

By relating the story of the land and its animals, we strive to draw away from the human-centered view of the world, so prevalent in the fields of architecture, history, and politics, and put forth a critical analysis of the multifaceted spatial processes that have taken place in a controversial land within a rather short time span of approximately 150 years.

The phrase "a land flowing with milk and honey" is one of the key images of abundance associated with the land of Palestine-Israel. It first appeared in the book of Exodus (3:17), when God spoke to Moses from the burning bush and promised to bring his people "unto a land flowing with milk and honey." The phrase is repeated in the bible on 21 occasions, mostly as a metaphor for plenitude.

Though small in size, the land of milk and honey has taken up great space in the imagination of Jews, Christians, and Muslims throughout the ages, who regarded it as a sacred geography, dreamed of it from afar, and longed for its pastoral, blessed landscapes. In all three religions, one finds written descriptions, poetry, and art, portraying the land through images of abundance: every man under his vine and fig tree, young women leading the flock, and young men harvesting the grapes. In these imaginary realms, the soil is fertile, its yield is oozing, and the earth is literally flowing with milk and honey.

In reality, however, there was often an enormous gap between the way in which people imagined the land from afar and the way they experienced it upon arrival. Testimonies such as that of George Pitt, an English traveler who visited Ottoman Palestine in the 19th century, were common:

> *My first strong impression, and I may say, my last, on beholding Palestine was one of astonishment. Can this be that glory of all lands—that promised land—the land flowing with milk and honey [...]? No! Surely not. I had pictured fertile plains and dewy meads, [...] cultivated lands [...] bringing forth luxuriant crops almost spontaneously. [...] Palestine, of all countries, is now desolate, barren, and accursed.*

Thus, although the land has supported the livelihoods of many people for hundreds and thousands of years, although it has been blessed with substantial agricultural production, diverse landscapes, and an extraordinary abundance of wildlife and flora biodiversity, those who came from afar often saw it as neglected, bare, and empty.

Beginning in the late 19th century and more vigorously in the 20th century, when European dominance in the Middle East was established and expanded, the landscape began to change, and with it—the peoples, animals, and resources. Through a series of initiatives in the fields of architecture, engineering, agronomy, veterinary medicine, and legislation, the country has undergone a far-reaching spatial and biological transformation. The British Mandate, the Zionist institutions, as well as the Israeli authorities, following the establishment of the state in 1948, have led proactive and wide-ranging spatial projects that utilized science, technology, and industrialization to recreate the land as a space of plenitude and, in effect, realize the vision of a Promised Land flowing with milk and honey. Decision-makers, ministers, clerks, scientists, engineers, architects, builders, and farmers—all were geared toward the fulfillment of the plenitude project.

Within a few decades, the "milk and honey" ideal—which had been, for generations, a vague divine promise, a utopian dream of a homeland, or an image of paradise at the end of days—became a plan of action. Phrases such as "making the wilderness bloom" and "conquering the desert" became official goals of government institutions, which enthusiastically redirected technological and budgetary resources to spatial engineering projects and agricultural development. "The land was created for human needs, and no place should be left desolate," wrote David Ben-Gurion, Israel's first prime minister, adding: "There is nothing more important and precious to man than to bring blossom to a desolate place, and this can be done with will, work, and scientific means."

Landscape reconstruction projects and biological interventions in animals and habitats were carried out based on an ethical code, ascribing "good" and "bad" values to scenery and animals: "good" being lush green forests, meadows, and agricultural fields, milk-yielding cows, white goats, and animals mentioned in the Bible, such as the oryx and the fallow-deer; "bad" being bare rocky mountains, marshes, camels, water buffaloes, bats, mosquitoes, and black goats. The outcome of these initiatives radically changed both the landscape and its inhabitants—humans (native Palestinians and Jewish newcomers) and animals (wild and domesticated) alike. Some areas underwent intensive forestation, fresh water springs were pumped and channeled to irrigate distant desert areas in the south, wetlands were drained and reconstructed as agricultural fields, and urbanization, infrastructure construction, and mechanized agriculture have transformed natural environments. All these had dramatic effects on the local wildlife. Livestock underwent far-reaching remodeling as well: camels and black goats suffered from severe grazing restrictions; cows' physiology was manipulated by cross-breeding procedures and diet regimes in order to improve milk yield; and the population of local honey bees was altogether replaced by an alternative, more prolific and sturdy, subspecies from Italy.

The Zionist plenitude project, which began in the last quarter of the 19th century and is ongoing to this day, is a complex set of worldviews, ideologies, and motivations. It is a political-national project, an economic enterprise, a refuge from persecution, and a unique mutation of colonial practices. Alongside all these, Zionism is a feeding plant—a systematic agenda aimed at supporting the unprecedented demographic growth that took place throughout the 20th century (from 757,000 people living between the Jordan

River and the Mediterranean Sea in 1922, to more than 13 million residents today; by 2050, the population is expected to top 20 million).

Although impressively successful in some respects, the "plenitude project" took heavy tolls. In addition to its harmful impact on the native inhabitants of the land, it also caused extensive environmental damage and led to the destruction of habitats and irreparable damage to the endemic fauna and flora.

Farm animals have also undergone mechanization processes, which turned their bodies into food-producing machines, literally manufacturing ever-growing amounts of milk and honey—the substance of plenitude. To a large extent, these processes and their outcomes have been a global phenomenon in the 20th century—an accelerated exploitation of nature for human needs using the modern tools of industrialization, urbanization, and construction; at the same time, the private case of Israel-Palestine is marked by an educated use of technologies for the realization of utopian projects and the implementation of a political agenda.

Unlike "human time," constantly rushing forward according to political events, economic processes, and social evolution, the environmental clock ticks slowly, advancing quietly through the ages; nonetheless, time passes—limestone erodes, rock is cut into terraces of vines and olive groves, rulers come and go; each bringing something with it: one brings the citron, the other—sugar cane, or water buffaloes. And then, time is accelerated: the sickle and plow are replaced by bulldozers, and the land is rapidly paved with asphalt and concrete. Suddenly one finds that the land has changed altogether.

Today, as the environmental consequences of modernization become apparent, the time has come to break away from anthropocentric perspectives and contemplate the effect we have on our closest neighbors, those who share the world with us.

To tell the story of this place, we therefore must move away from the world of humans and focus on the earth itself. We shall thus recount the story of animals—those that were extinct with the destruction of their habitats, those that barely survived, and those that thrive in the built-up human world. We shall tell the story of farm animals, whose numbers have dramatically risen under the rule of man, and the varied, strange ways in which we dictate the course of their lives. We will tell of this land, which so many have dreamed of and longed for, and how it found itself torn, crushed, asphalted, teeming with concrete and toxins, its streams contaminated, its lakes dry. The land is witness, and the animals will testify. This is their story.

Land
Chapter 1

Geography.

Our story begins with the place: with the grains of sand making up the soil; with the unfolding landscape—the real scenery as well as the imaginary; with the stories recounted about sand and land and landscape. Our story begins with the place: the place that has always been here, even before people started building stone houses and believing in various odd gods—the mountains, valleys, wadis, sun and rain, plants and animals.

The place is the western end of the Fertile Crescent, the eastern end of the Mediterranean Sea, a stretch of land connecting three continents—Africa, Asia, and Europe. As a linking space, it bridges the fauna and flora of these three continents, bringing together diverse climates, conditions which made it possible for camels to live in the country's arid south, while brown bears lived in the cold northern mountains, only 300 km apart. Different human species lived here side by side, and next to Lake Huleh and the Jordan River, the first stone houses were erected. This is where animals were first domesticated, as was the mother-of-wheat (wild emmer).

The country's southern region is a desert with scarce fresh water sources. This is where the region's great strip of desert ends. In the east, along a geological fault, a chain of small lakes was formed, the Jordan River running between them from north to south: Lake Huleh, the Sea of Galilee, the Dead Sea. The country's center is cut by a range of stone-covered mountains, from Judea to the Galilee. There are perennial streams and seasonal streams, and the sea lies on the west side. Along the coastal strip, from Rafah to

Lebanon, sand dunes slope downward; and the lowlands are home to red loam and swamps on the riverbanks. Only four valleys lie between the mountains, the desert, and the sea, and their soil is good for agriculture.

There are years of drought and years of abundant rain, and the sun here is scorching. Agricultural fields cover the hill slopes or are hewn on terraces on the mountainsides—olive groves, grape vineyards, pomegranate and fig trees. Dates grow in the dry south, wheat fields and barley in the plains, and the occasional vegetables and legumes all around. In addition to the fields, livestock is also raised—goats, sheep, and cattle, camels, horses, and donkeys, mules, and honey bees. In the 6th century BC, the Persians brought the citron to Palestine, and in the 8th century—the Arabs brought lemons, oranges, sugarcane, as well as the water buffalo—Jamus, in the local lingo.

Amid the people, the fields, and the farm animals, one may discern manifestations of primal nature that seem to have been here from time immemorial: the sand dunes, the beaches, mountains, and forests of oak and terebinth trees, streams, wadis, and swamps. In the past, there were hippopotami, wild donkeys and lions here, as well as bears and ostriches, leopards and cheetahs, alligators and wild bulls—all now gone. They existed side by side with ibexes, fallow deer, wild asses, rams, foxes, wolves, jackals, all kinds of snakes and turtles (sea turtles, freshwater turtles, and land turtles); scorpions, beetles, butterflies, and wild bees (1,100 species); hyenas, gazelles, roe deer, otters, mongoose, wildcats, wild boar, fruit bats and insect bats; and fowl—storks, herons, cranes, ibises, egrets, various ducks, eagles, barn owls, falcons, crows, and bulbuls—a long list that could have filled this entire book.

Gili Merin, *Eretz (Land)*, 2020 »

Many travelers toured the land and recorded their impressions in writing. Approximately 3,500 journals written by tourists, pilgrims, soldiers, explorers, and officials are known, about 2,000 of them were written in the late 19th century. These manuscripts may be assembled to form a jigsaw puzzle spanning impressions of a place throughout the ages.

A Journey from Aleppo to Jerusalem at Easter
Henry Maundrell, 1697

All along this day's travel from Kane Leban to Beer, and also as far as we could see round, the country discover'd a quite different face from what it had before, presenting nothing to the view in most places, but naked rocks, mountains, and precipices. At sight of which, pilgrims are apt to be much astonished and baulk'd in their expectations; finding that country in such an inhospitable condition, concerning whose pleasantness and plenty they had before form'd in their minds such high idea's from the description given of it in the word of God. [...] For it is obvious for any one to observe, that these rocks, and hills must have been anciently cover'd with earth, and cultivated, and made to contribute to the maintenance of the inhabitants, no less than if the country had been all plain. [...] For the husbanding of these mountains, their manner was to gather up the stones, and

Henry Maundrell (1665-1701), a Church of England clergyman and chaplain of the Levant Company in Aleppo, Syria, left for Jerusalem in 1697, accompanied by 14 fellow countrymen, to celebrate Easter there. His journey took him down the Syrian and Lebanese coasts, passing through Acre, the Jezreel Valley, and Samaria, and finally reaching Jerusalem.

place them in several lines, along the sides of the hills, in form of a wall. By such borders they supported the mould from tumbling, or being washed down; and form'd many beds of excellent soil, rising gradually one above another, from the bottom to the top of the mountains.

Of this form of culture you see evident footsteps, wherever you go in all the mountains of Palestine. Thus the very rocks were made fruitful. And perhaps there is no spot of ground in this whole land, that was not formerly improv'd, to the production of something or other, ministering to the sustenance of human life. For, than the plain countries, nothing can be more fruitful, whether for the production of corn or cattle, and consequently of milk. The hills, though improper for all cattle, except goats, yet being disposed into such beds as are afore described, served very well to bear corn, melons, goards, cucumbers, and such like garden stuff, which makes the principal food of these countries for several months in the year. The most rocky parts of all, which could not well be adjusted in that manner for the production of corn, might yet serve for the plantation of vines and olive trees; which delight to extract, the one its fatness, the other its sprightly juice, chiefly out of such dry and flinty places. And the great plain joining to the dead sea, which, by reason of its saltness, might be thought unserviceable both for cattle, corn, olives, and vines, had yet its proper usefulness, for the nourishment of bees, and for the fabrick of honey; of which Josephus gives us his testimony *De Bell. Jud. lib. 5. cap. 4.* And I have reason to believe it; because when I was there, I perceived in many places a smell of honey and wax, as strong as if one had been in an apiary.

The Land of Israel: A Journal of Travels in Palestine
Henry Baker Tristram, 1863–64

February 23d.

Another cloudless day smiled on our ride to Nablous, through a country yet more beautified by spring than the vales of Benjamin yesterday. The flowers were even more abundant; the scarlet anemone, cyclamen, and, above all, the little pink lychnis, combined to spread a red carpet over the land, while patches of blue pimpernel and veronica, with tufts of yellow ranunculus, prettily variegated the pattern, and the green barley formed a rich turf under the olive-trees. Through the length of the once bare plain of Mokhna (Shechem), many a yoke of dwarf oxen were lazily dragging the simple wooden plough, guided by a still more lazy Bedouin with one hand, while his other plied the goad, and women with asses were bringing sacks of wheat from the hills for seed. Though the barley was four inches high, the wheat was only just being sown. The ground is scratched with a wooden plough to a depth of not more than six inches, and so light is the soil, filled with small stones, that no harrowing is required—the corn is scattered, and at once raked roughly in. The earth is red, or red brown, very friable, and having the appearance of great richness, which its produce does not belie; for no manure is used beyond the anemones and stubble which are ploughed in. [...]

Henry Baker Tristram (1822–1906), a learned English parson, naturalist, traveler, and ornithologist, visited Palestine three times between 1858 and 1872. His books—in which, among other things, he surveyed the native species of flora and fauna—promoted the study of Holy Land geography and contributed to identification of loci mentioned in the Bible.

February 24th.

Profiting by our recollections of the Cave of Adullam, I took a Samaritan guide to revisit Gerizim, with U. and S. while the rest of the party went on to Jenin. The artery between Northern and Southern Palestine could to-day be seen to full advantage, narrow, long, and well wooded, watered by its gushing rills, with its orchards of orange, palm, and fig; but conspicuous above the rest were apricots, almonds, and peaches, now one beautiful sheet of pink or white blossom, creeping up the southern mountain's side, while olive groves clad Ebal's lower slopes, and the smooth-leaved cactus almost covered its rocky sides above.

PALESTINE.

Report on Immigration, Land Settlement and Development.

By
Sir JOHN HOPE SIMPSON, C.I.E.

1930.

Presented by the Secretary of State for the Colonies to Parliament by Command of His Majesty.
October, 1930.

LONDON:
PRINTED AND PUBLISHED BY HIS MAJESTY'S STATIONERY OFFICE.
To be purchased directly from H.M. STATIONERY OFFICE at the following addresses.
Adastral House, Kingsway, London, W.C.2; 120, George Street, Edinburgh;
York Street, Manchester; 1, St. Andrew's Crescent, Cardiff;
15, Donegall Square West, Belfast,
or through any Bookseller.

1930.

Price 3s. 0d. net.

Cmd. 3686.

Chapter I
Palestine: The Country and the Climate

*

(a) The Hill Country

Soil and Agriculture

The cultivated land in the Hills varies very largely both in depth and quality of the soil. In the valleys there are stretches of fertile land, which will grow sesame as a summer crop. On the hillsides the soil is shallow and infertile, and the extent of land hunger is evident from the fact that every available plot of soil is cultivated, even when it is so small that the plough cannot be employed. There cultivation is carried on with the mattock and the hoe. The harvest of such plots, even in a favourable year, is exceedingly small—in general it seems doubtful whether such cultivation can pay. On the other hand, even the most rocky hillsides support trees, especially olives, and if capital were available, many of the cultivators of these exiguous and infertile plots would be able to gain a livelihood by cultivation of fruit trees and of olives. These cultivators have, however, no capital, and cannot afford to forgo even the meagre crops obtained, for the four or five years which are required before fruit trees render a return. In the case of the olive, the period before a return may be expected is much longer.

"The Hope-Simpson Report," addressing "immigration, land settlement and development," is the official account and summary of recommendations made by a British committee headed by Sir John Hope Simpson, sent to Palestine by the Secretary of State for the Colonies following the Arab revolt that broke out in August 1929. In the Report, the committee recommended restricting Jewish immigration to Palestine due to the country's limited economic capacity.

Irrigation

There is little irrigation in the hill country. Here and there are springs which afford a supply for the irrigation of a small area, but, taken as a whole, the country is arid and the crops depend on rain. It is possible that a hydrographic survey might disclose further water supplies, and scientific treatment might also improve the yield from existing springs. It is stated that during the War the Engineers of the Army of Occupation were able very largely to increase the supply from springs in certain places.

Development

In the best case, however, it is impossible that the general character of the cultivation in the Hill country can be radically changed, except in so far as fruit can be made to replace grain. Something might be done to improve the soil and to reform agricultural methods, were capital available. The use of manures and provision of better seed would doubtless result in some improvement of the yield. But from the point of view of agriculture, the Hill country will always remain an unsatisfactory proposition.

(b) The Five Plains

1.—The Maritime Plain

[…] A reference to Map No. 2 will show that the Maritime Plain is taken to be the area between the coast and the hills up to the 150 metre contour, running from Eafa in the south up to Haifa in the north. Ordinarily the Maritime Plain is treated as running from Rafa to RasenNaqura, on the Syrian border. The reason for the present division lies in the difference in the class of soil of the plains north and south of Haifa. The latter portion of the plain is the tract which contains the great mass of windblown sand, so suitable for orange cultivation. The former is in the main a heavy black soil quite unsuited for oranges. [...]

2.—*The Acre Plain*

[...] This is the coastal plain lying north of Haifa and running up between the sea and the hills as far as the Syrian border. [...] This plain is in the main composed of an alluvial deposit, rather heavy in character. There is a small area of windblown sand suitable for plantations, but, generally, the type of developed cultivation will be mixed farming with irrigation. There is ample water from springs and streams. A large area in this plain is held by the Bayside Land Corporation—a Jewish corporation.

Haifa Harbour

The future of this tract will be advantageously affected by the construction of the Haifa Harbour. Work is already in progress and is advancing rapidly. The harbour will greatly assist the development of the export trade in oranges, and perhaps other agricultural products. [...]

3.—*The Vale of Esdraelon*

[...] The evidence as to the fertility of the Vale of Esdraelon and the state of its prosperity in the hands of the Arabs, before the extensive purchases made by the Jews, is conflicting. In his report on the administration of Palestine, 192025, at p. 35, Sir Herbert Samuel wrote: "...The whole aspect of the valley has been changed. The wooden fauts of the villages, gradually giving place to redroofed cottages, are dotted along the slopes; the plantations of rapidly growing eucalyptus trees already begin to give a new character to the landscape; in the spring the fields of vegetables or of cereals cover many miles of the land, and what five years ago was little better than a wilderness is being transformed before our eyes into a smiling countryside."

On the other hand, Dr. Strahorn writes in his report [...]: "...Up to within recent years the land was cultivated from the Arab villages, located round the rim of the Plain. Cereals together with minor garden areas around the villages constituted the Arab cropping system. In very recent years considerable areas of land have passed under the control of Jewish colonies and villages; gardens and orchards are now dotting the former expanse of grainfields..."

Results of Jewish Settlement

The results of Jewish colonisation of the Vale of Esdraelon are varied. In some villages there are clear signs of success; in others, the opposite is the case. The village of Afuleh, which the American Zionist Commonwealth boomed as the Chicago of Palestine, is a sea of thistles through which one travels for long distances. A plague of field mice, which has done extensive damage to both Jewish and Arab cultivation in the Vale during the present year was officially stated to be due to the fact that 30,000 dunams of the land held by the Jews are derelict and covered with weeds. It is also a fact that in a number of villages the tithes paid by the Jews are considerably below those paid by the Arabs who formerly cultivated those villages.

Its Past

It is a mistake to assume that the Vale of Esdraelon was a wilderness before the arrival of the Jewish settlers and that it is now a paradise. A very large amount of money has been spent by the various Jewish agencies, and great improvements have been made. The work that has been done, especially in the direction of drainage and the introduction of new and improved methods of agriculture is highly valuable. There can be little doubt that in time, the application of capital, science, and labour will result in general success. It is, however, unjust to the poverty-stricken fellah' who has been removed from these lands that the suggestion should continually be made that he was a useless cumberer of the ground and produced nothing from it. It should be quite obvious that this is not the fact. In ancient times Esdraelon was the granary, and by the Arabs is still regarded as the most fertile tract of Palestine. The soreness felt owing to the sale of large areas by the absentee Sursock family to the Jews and the displacement of the Arab tenants is still acute. It was evident on every occasion of discussion with the Arabs, both effendi and fellahin.

Soils

The soil of the valley is generally an alluvial clay, highly suitable to cereal cultivation. Across the Vale at one place there is a belt of residual soil, even heavier than the alluvial of the rest of the valley. Both in the cultivation of cereals and in that of fodder crops the soil responds to high farming.

4.—*The Huleh Plain*

[…] The Huleh Plain is the most northerly part of Palestine, to the east of the country, and lies to the north of the Lake of Tiberias. Its area is reported by the Director of Surveys as 191,000 metric dunams; of this extent 126,000 dunams are cultivable. […]

Character

The Huleh Plain may be divided into three parts. In the north there is rich alluvial cultivable land; south of this there is a large marshy area covered with papyrus reeds, the haunt of the wild boar and the grazing ground of numerous water buffaloes which are the property of the Bedu tribes of the neighbourhood. South of this again is the Lake of Merom, through which the Jordan flows southwards to Lake Tiberias. The Lake and marsh are caused by a ridge of basalt across the Jordan Valley. If this ridge were cleared away or the river deepened, the whole valley could be drained and considerable areas of land made available for irrigated cultivation.

Marsh Area

There are widely varying estimates of the extent of the marsh and of the extent of the lake. […] No survey of the marsh area has been made, nor is one possible, except by air, until the marsh is drained. It will be safe to assume that, excluding the cultivation of the Arabs in that area, there is still an area of some 25,000 to 30,000 metric dunams of marsh land available for reclamation. Were the Lake also drained a further 9,000 or 10,000 metric dunams would be rendered cultivable. The soil of the whole Huleh Plain is exceedingly fertile. It is indeed said to be the most fertile soil in Palestine.

5.—*The Plain of the Jordan*

[...] The land in the north of the Jordan Valley is very fertile; in the south, with irrigation, it will grow all kinds of tropical fruits, and early vegetables. Properly developed the Jordan Valley might prove a great source of wealth to the country. In ancient times it undoubtedly supported a large population.

(c) The Beersheba Region

Area

This is estimated at 3,200,000 dunams, of which 1,500,000 are cultivable. The figures are in fact pure guesswork, as is admitted by the Director of Surveys. [...] Given the possibility of irrigation there is practically an inexhaustible supply of cultivable land in the Beersheba area. Without irrigation, the country cannot be developed. Up to the present time there has been no organised attempt to ascertain whether there is or is not an artesian supply of water. If there prove to be such a supply the problem of providing agricultural land for the Palestine population and, indeed, for a large number of immigrant settlers, will be easy of solution.

PALESTINE

MAP No. 6.

SCALE 1:250,000

REFERENCE

- Jewish National Fund Land
- P.I.C.A. Land
- Other Jewish Land
- Land Purchased by Contracts (boundaries not yet defined)
- Land not yet Divided

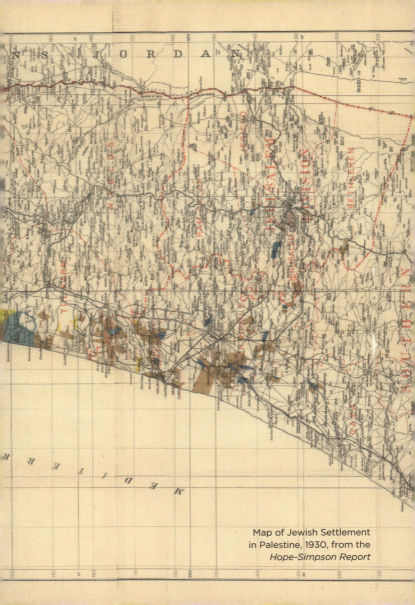

Map of Jewish Settlement in Palestine, 1930, from the *Hope-Simpson Report*

Holy Land.

Pilgrimages to the Holy Land have been customary in the Christian world for generations. These travels first gained popularity in the 4th century CE, when Christianity became the official religion of the Roman Empire. A journey of special note was that of Saint Helena, Emperor Constantine's mother, who visited Judea in 325 CE and identified many holy places associated with Jesus and his disciples, including the place of the Crucifixion and the Holy Sepulcher. Based on these spots, a "holy geography" was created, which spanned the map of holy sites and pilgrimage routes.

Although not a religious obligation, pilgrimage is considered a sign of piousness and devotion, and is often accompanied by a mystical vein of union with the Creator. The physical territory to which believers traveled was always called the "Holy Land," regardless of the administrative names given by the land's ever-changing residents or rulers. The travelers' memories, their written, illustrated or oral impressions, often differ from the landscape of the real place, as they concentrate on description of the holy sites and enveloped by an aura of sanctity and revelation. In some instances, the land is described as is, with its modest beauty and perils—but at all time, by virtue of its being a "holy land," it is regarded as a place not bound by definitions of natural and political borders: an a-geographical sphere, a super-place, a spatial incarnation of spirituality and salvation.

St. Paula of Rome
4th century

> Behold, in this little nook of the earth the Founder of the heavens was born; here He was wrapped in swaddling clothes, beheld by the shepherds, shown by the star, adored by the wise men.

> But in the village of Christ, as we said before, all is rusticity, and except for psalms, silence. Whithersoever you turn yourself, the ploughman, holding the plough-handle, sings Alleluia; the perspiring reaper diverts himself with psalms, and the vine-dresser sings some of the songs of David while he trims the vine with his curved knife. These are the ballads of this country, these are the love-songs, as they are commonly called; these are whistled by the shepherds, and are the implements of the husbandman. Indeed, we do not think of what we are doing or of how we look, but see only that for which we are longing.

St. Paula of Rome (347–404 CE)— a Roman widow of noble descent who lived a rich matron's life—decided, for reasons of religious piety, to divide all her property and travel to Palestine with her daughter. The two settled in Bethlehem, where Paula passed away some twenty years later. Her memoirs were recorded by St. Jerome.

The Piacenza Pilgrim
560–570

This province [of Nazareth] is like a paradise, in corn and produce it is like Egypt; but it excels in wine and oil, fruits, and honey. Millet, too, is there unnaturally tall, higher than the stature of a tall man.

From Nazareth we came to Mount Tabor, which mountain rises from the centre of the plain: it is formed of productive earth, and is six miles in circuit, three in ascent, and has a plain of one mile on the top. Upon it are three churches [...]. Thence we came to the city of Tiberias, in which are hot baths of salt water; for the water of the sea itself is sweet.

The Piacenza Pilgrim, sometimes referred to as Antoninus the Martyr, was born in the city of Piacenza in northern Italy. The account of his travels in the Holy Land is rich in fantastic tales. His journal was originally published in 1640.

Mt. Tabor, illustration by J.D. Woodward, from the book *Picturesque Palestine*, 1881–84

The Best Divisions for Knowledge of the Regions
Shams al-Din (al-Muqaddasi), 985

Tabariyya (Tiberias) is the capital of Jordan [...]. It is situated between the mountain and the lake, cramped, with suffocating heat in summer, and unhealthy. [...] There are eight hot baths here needing no fuel, along with numerous basins of hot water. The mosque is large and fine, and stands in the marketplace; its floor is laid in pebbles, and the building rests on pillars of joined stone. [...]

Near Tiberias are boiling springs that supply most of the hot baths of the town. A conduit has been laid to each bath, so that the steam heats the rooms of the building, and thus there is no need for a fire. In the first compartment you enter, cold water is at hand which may be mingled with the hot in the amount to cleanse oneself, and there are lavatories for the Ablution with this same water. In this area are other hot springs called el-Hamma (hot waters); should one suffering from mange, ulcers, or tumours, or other maladies bathe himself here for three days, and then bathe himself in another spring which is cold, he will be cured, if God wills it. I have heard the people of Tiberias relate that all around these springs there used to be bath houses, each house for the relief of a specific ailment; anyone with that disease who bathed there would be cured; these bath houses were there right down to the time of Aristotle.

Shams al-Din, better known as al-Muqaddasi, was born in Jerusalem in 945 CE. His treatise, published in 985 CE, includes impressions and observations of his twenty-year long travels throughout the Islamic empire.

Pilgrimage of the Russian Abbot Daniel in the Holy Land
Abbot Daniel, ca. 1106–1107

Mount Tabor is a marvelous work of God that one cannot describe, so beautiful it is, so lofty and so grand; it has the appearance of a haycock, and rises majestically in the midst of a magnificent plain; it is isolated from all other mountains, and a river flows through the plain at its feet. All sorts of trees grow upon its slopes—olive, fig, and carob trees in large numbers. It is higher than the other mountains round, and is absolutely isolated from them; its circumference is considerable, and it rises majestically in the midst of a plain like a carefully rounded haycock. Its height is such that it is four bow-shots from its summit to its base, and more than eight firing from the base to the summit. It is rocky, and this makes the ascent troublesome and difficult; it has to be climbed zigzag by a very arduous way. Starting at the third hour of the day, and climbing with vigour, we hardly reached the summit of this holy mountain at the ninth hour. On the highest point, to the south-east, is an elevated spot like a little rocky hill, terminating in a conical peak. This is the place of the Transfiguration of Christ our God. At the present day there is a fine church dedicated to the Transfiguration; and another at its side, to the north, is dedicated to the Holy Prophets Moses and Elias. [...]

From Mount Tabor to Nazareth it is five versts, two over the plain and three over the mountain, where the road is troublesome, narrow and very

Abbot Daniel was a Russian pilgrim who visited many of the holy places in Palestine in the early 12th century and described them at length. His accounts are an important source that sheds light on the country's condition in the years following its conquest by the Crusaders. His manuscript also includes nature and landscape descriptions: panthers and wild asses living in the Judean Desert, lions in the Jordan Valley, and date-palms growing in Jericho.

arduous; impious Saracens, whose villages are scattered over the mountains and the plain, issue from their homes and massacre travelers on those terrible heights. It is dangerous to go across without a good escort, which we lacked this time, for we were only eight persons, without arms. But having put our trust in God, protected by His mercy, and assisted by the prayers of Our Lady, the Holy Virgin, we arrived safe and sound at the holy city of Nazareth…

The Valley of Nazareth, illustration by Harry Fenn, from the book *Picturesque Palestine*, 1881–84

Burchard of Mount Sion
1275–1285

The whole of the Holy Land was, and is at this day, the best of all lands, albeit some who have not carefully regarded it say the contrary. It is very fertile in corn, which is tilled and grown with scarce any labour. The soil yields many herbs. Fennel, sage, rue, and roses grow everywhere of their own accord on the plains. Cotton grows on certain shrubs, which are about as tall as a man's knee [...]. Sugar-canes also grow there. These are like common canes, but bigger. Within they are hollow, but full of a porous substance like that which one finds in rods of elder-wood. This substance is very moist. The canes are gathered, cut in lengths of half a palm, and so are crushed in the press. The juice squeezed out of them is boiled in copper boilers, and, when thickened, is collected in baskets made of slender twigs. Soon after this it becomes dry and hard, and this is how sugar is made. Before it dries, a liquor oozes from it, called honey of sugar, which is very-delicious, and good for flavouring cakes. Moreover, they cut the canes into pieces as long as a man's finger. They bury these pieces at spring-time in damp ground, and from them new canes grow, two out of each one, from either side of the knot. This is how they plant them.

You must know that in this land one hardly ever finds pears, or apples, or cherries [...]. Some fruits are brought from Damascus, but they are quite soft, and cannot last long, because of the great heat. [...]

Burchard of Mount Sion, a 13th-century Dominican friar, embarked on a long journey to the Holy Land, visiting Egypt, Cilicia (Armenia), and Syria along the way. For a decade, he lived in the Franciscan Monastery on Mount Sion, Jerusalem, hence his nickname. His accounts stand out in their tolerant approach and accurate, reliable descriptions.

There is also the fruit called peach, whereof an exceeding good preserve is made at Acre. There is also another fruit, called apples of paradise (banana), a very fine fruit.

There are many vines in the Holy Land, and there would be more, but that the Saracens, who now hold the land, drink no wine, except some of them in secret, […] and destroy the vines, all save a few, perhaps, who dwell near Christians, and grow them for profit, that they may sell them to Christians. The wine of the Holy Land is very good and noble, especially round about Bethlehem, in the Valley of Rephaim, and so on. Figs and pomegranates, honey and oil, and herbs of all sorts, such as gourds and cucumbers, and many other fruits, abound there.

Wild-boars, roes, hares, partridges, and quails are so plentiful that it is a wonder to see them. There are many lions there, and bears, and diverse kinds of wild beasts; moreover there are infinite numbers of camels and dromedaries, stags, buffaloes, and, in short, there are therein all the good things in the world, and the land flows with milk and honey. But they who dwell therein I cannot call brave men, but it contains the worst and basest sort of sinners, so that it is wonderful that the land should endure them.

The Inner Life of Syria, Palestine, and the Holy Land
Isabel Burton, 1875

Everywhere this day the earth was beautifully green, and carpeted with wild flowers. The air was fresh and balmy, and laden with the sweet scents of spring—grass, herbs, trees, and flowers. We passed the black tents of the Arabs, who gave me milk to drink; and also one well, where we watered the horses. In the Sahl, or Plain, of Esdraelon, there were thousands of storks, which were quite undisturbed by our appearance, and let us ride through them like a flock of sheep; but when they rose to fly altogether, they made such a fearful noise, and looked so large, that my horse took fright, and ran away for about a mile. The sky was so blue, the mountains and plains looked so beautiful, the birds, insects, the wild flowers, the fresh balmy breeze, sweet smells, and gentle sun, the black tents, all combined to make one glad to be alive. The senses were satisfied, and it was a day of physical enjoyment, of real Kayf, so few of which fall to the lot of Man. However, when all is said, nothing is perfect—I was alone!

Lady Isabel Burton (1831–1896) was wife and partner of explorer and writer Richard Francis Burton. She toured the Holy Land with her husband and published her memoirs of the journey.

Bernhard von Breydenbach (ca. 1440–1497) was a politician in the Electorate of Mainz, a doctor, and the editor of the first German guide to medicinal herbs. His *Peregrinatio in terram sanctam* (Pilgrimage to the Holy Land, 1486) is a travel report based on his pilgrimage to the Holy Land, written in Latin with Dominican monk Martin Roth and illustrated with wood engravings by **Erhard Reuwich**, who accompanied Breydenbach on the pilgrimage. »

070 ‹Holy Land›

072 ‹ Holy Land ›

Breydenbach's map, 1486: the Holy Land, with Jerusalem at the center

Illustration from Bernhard von Breydenbach's book, 1486; original caption: "These animals were faithfully portrayed as seen in the Holy Land. From top to bottom: giraffe, crocodile, Indian goat, unicorn, camel, salamander; the last animal's nam is unknown" »

Ces bestes Icy soubz pourtraictes sont comme nous les auõs veues en la terre saicte

Taxonomies.

In the mid-19th century, Palestine saw a new kind of traveler—not only devout believers following in the footsteps of Christ, but also scientific experts, who came to map the land, examine its soil, and catalogue its fauna and flora in the spirit of the colonial era.

The Land of Israel: A Journal of Travels in Palestine
Henry Baker Tristram, 1863–64

> We never met with so many wild animals as on one of these days. First of all, a wild-boar got out of some scrub close to us, as we were ascending the valley. U. sent a ball into him, but he carried it off. Then a deer was started below, ran up the cliff, and wound along the ledge, passing close to us. Then a large ichneumon almost crossed my feet, and ran into a cleft; and, while endeavouring to trace him, I was amazed to see a brown Syrian bear clumsily but rapidly clamber down the rocks and cross the ravine. He was, however, far too cautious to get within hailing distance of any of the riflemen. While working the ropes above, we could see the gazelles tripping lightly at the bottom of the valley, quite out of reach and sight of our companions at the foot of the cliff. L., who was below, also saw an otter, which came out of the water, and stood and looked at him for a minute with surprise. Five great griffons were shot by S. and U., the preparation of whose highly-scented skins was no light task for the taxidermists.

THE SURVEY

OF

WESTERN PALESTINE.

THE FAUNA AND FLORA OF PALESTINE.

BY

H. B. TRISTRAM, LL.D., D.D., F.R.S.,

CANON OF DURHAM.

The Survey of Western Palestine is a collection of surveys carried out by the Palestine Exploration Fund (PEF) between 1872 and 1877. It includes reports and detailed maps of the topography, ethnography, and archaeology of the land, as well as a volume dedicated to the fauna and flora, written by Henry Baker Tristram.

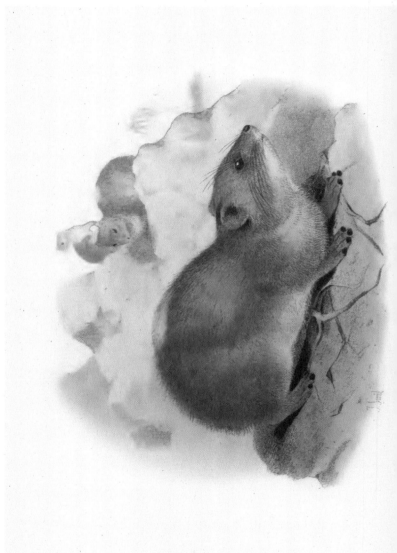

THE
FAUNA AND FLORA OF PALESTINE.

MAMMALIA.

ORDER, PACHYDERMATA.

FAMILY, HYRACIDÆ.

1. *Hyrax Syriacus.* Hemp. and Ehr. Symb. Phys. Mamm. Pl. 2. Coney. Heb. שָׁפָן. Arab. طبسن, *Tubsun*, or الوبر, *el Wabr* (in Sinai).

PLATE I.

This singular little Mammal, neither ruminant nor rodent, but which is placed by systematists among the *Ungulata*, near the Rhinoceros, is one of the many peculiarly African forms which occur in Palestine. It is not uncommon round the shores of the Dead Sea, but is rare in the rest of the country, and not known in Lebanon. It is found throughout the Sinaitic Peninsula generally, but is not known to extend further into Arabia or Western Asia. It is represented by a very closely allied species in Abyssinia, and by another rather larger at the Cape. Several species, or varieties, occur in Eastern Africa, but this is the only one known beyond the limits of that continent. Its Hebrew name means 'the hider,' and its timid, cautious habits, and defenceless character are referred to in Scripture. The Syrian Coney is marked by a yellow dorsal spot on its otherwise uniformly tawny fur. It is scarcely so large as a full-grown Rabbit. Its teeth and toes resemble those of the Hippopotamus in miniature. It lives exclusively among the rocks in Wâdys, not generally burrowing, but utilizing fissures in the cliffs, where it has its inaccessible home, coming forth to feed only at sunset and at dawn.

even seen it on the Mount of Olives, close to Jerusalem. It is frequently mentioned in Scripture, and rendered 'Roe' in our translation; and is a favourite symbol both of fleetness and of beauty. There are many species or geographical races of Gazelle, some of them difficult to discriminate. The Dorcas Gazelle is found from Algeria through Egypt, and thence extends into Arabia and Syria.

17. *Gazella arabica.* (?) Ehrenb. Symb. Phys. Mamm. 1 r.

This species, larger than the Dorcas Gazelle, is found in the desert country east of Jordan. I had formerly identified it with Ehrenberg's species from South Arabia; but Sir Victor Brooke, while recognising its distinctness, is inclined to believe it another race, less widely separated from *G. dorcas.* The Persian *G. subgutturosa* and the Indian *G. benettii* are distinct.

Caprinæ.

18. *Capra hircus.* L. Syst. Nat. i., p. 94. The Goat. Heb. עָפִיר, He-goat; עֵז, She-goat. Arab. معز, *Ma'z.*

The Goat is more abundant in this hilly and scantily watered country than the Sheep, and constitutes its chief wealth. There are many different breeds or races. The ordinary Black Goat of Syria, universal throughout the country, with pendent ears a foot long, hanging down far below the recurved horns, has been distinguished as *Capra mambrica*, L. Syst. Nat. i., 95. The Mohair-Goat (*Capra angorensis*, L. Syst. Nat. i., 94) is occasionally bred in some parts of the north of Palestine.

19. *Capra beden.* Wagn. Schreb. Saug. V. a. 1303. (*C. sinaitica.* Ehrenb. Symb. Phys., t. 18.) Ibex. Heb. יְעֵלִים. Arab. بدن, *Beden.*

PLATE II.

The Syrian Ibex, or Beden, is still found, not only in the ravines of Moab, but in the wilderness of Judæa, near the Dead Sea. I have procured several specimens on both sides of Jordan. It is not now known in the north or in Lebanon, where I have found its teeth in cave-breccia, along with flint implements. The Beden is of a much lighter fawn colour than the European Ibex, with horns much more slender and recurved, wrinkled and knotted on the front face only. It is the 'Wild Goat' of Scripture.

is found in Egypt, Nubia, Abyssinia, Arabia, and the Persian and Indian deserts. In habits it differs from its congener, sweeping the desert plains rather than soaring over the mountain cliffs.

FAMILY, CERTHIIDÆ.

108. *Tichodroma muraria.* (Linn. Syst. Nat. i., p. 184.) Wall Creeper.

The beautiful Creeper, the 'Butterfly Bird' of the French, is common throughout the year in all the rocky gorges of Central and Northern Palestine, from the glens opening on the plain of Gennesaret to the highest cliffs of Lebanon. No ornithological sight is more interesting than the movements of this richly coloured bird as it flits along the face of a line of cliffs, spreading its brilliant crimson wings at each sidling jerk.

The Wall Creeper is found in the mountain regions of all Central and Southern Europe and Asia, from Spain to the Himalayas and China.

FAMILY, NECTARINIIDÆ.

109. *Cinnyris oseæ.* Bonap. Comptes Rendus. xlii., Pt. 2, p. 765. Palestine Sun-Bird.

PLATE VIII.

To the naturalist this is perhaps the most interesting species of the whole Palestinian Avifauna. In the first place, it belongs to a truly tropical family. In the second place, it is absolutely peculiar, so far as we know, to the Holy Land, and within its limits is confined to a very narrow strip of territory; and lastly, we must travel very far from Palestine east or south to find another representative of the numerous Sun-bird family. We must go either to India or far up the Nile into Nubia. At least 135 species of Sun-bird are known, confined entirely to the warmer parts of the Old World, to Southern Asia and all its islands, as far as North Australia, to Africa, south of the Sahara, and to the Mascarene Islands and Madagascar. They are unknown in the New World and in Oceania. In habits they

Lake of Galilee, where our Cormorant is very common. I discovered in 1881 a great breeding colony of Pygmy Cormorant in the reedy islets of the Lake of Antioch, where this bird was nesting in hundreds in society with the Snake Bird of Africa (*Plotus levaillantii*), and the Common Tern (*Sterna hirundo*), hatching about the end of May.

The Pygmy Cormorant is found in South-east Europe from the Danube southwards, in North-east Africa, and Southern Asia, as far as India, Java, and Borneo; but it does not appear to extend towards China.

227. *Pelecanus onocrotalus.* Linn. Syst. Nat. i., p. 215. Roseate Pelican. Hebr., קָאַת. Arab., جمل البحر, *Djemel el bahr*, اِبُ جراب, *Abu djirab*.

The Roseate Pelican is frequently found on the Sea of Galilee, though I never myself was fortunate enough to find it there until my visit in 1881. I also observed a flock of this species mingled with the next off Tyre.

The Roseate Pelican has a limited range from the Danube to the east of the Mediterranean, North-east Africa, and Syria, to the Black Sea and the Caspian.

228. *Pelecanus crispus.* Bruch. *Isis*, 1832, p. 1109. Dalmatian Pelican.

The Dalmatian Pelican is more abundant than its congener. I have seen an immense flock pursuing their singularly gyrating flight near Mount Carmel. It is generally to be found at Lake Huleh.

The winter limits of the Dalmatian are much the same as those of the Roseate Pelican. But it extends further to the eastward, being frequent in Western India.

FAMILY, PLOTIDÆ.

229. *Plotus levaillantii.* Licht. Verz. Doubl., p. 87. African Darter.

PLATE XIII.

Though I have not actually obtained this bird within the confines of Palestine proper, yet, as I have discovered a great breeding colony on

The Land of Israel and Southern Syria: The Travel Book
Isaiah Press, 1921

The Animals of the Land
The animals of our land are of a mixed nature. One may find animals belonging to two different regions, to cold lands and to warm countries. In the Upper Galilee, the Golan Heights, and on Mt. Hermon one encounters animals of the northern lands, while in the central and southern regions—species that live in Sinai, Egypt, the Nubian Desert, and Libya. Of the animals of Transjordan, in Hauran and the desert, some species resemble the animals of Arabia, Mesopotamia, and India.

Mammals
The mammals belonging to the cold regions are: the Syrian brown bear, previously very common in the country's south, can now be found only in the Lebanon ranges, on Mt. Hermon, and in Jabel el-Mshakah (the Ladder of Tyre) between Tyre and Acre; the badger, river otter, the seal living on our shores, the lynx, the skunk in the Lebanon range, the hedgehog, the shrew-mouse, the squirrel, the marmot, the dwarf-hamster, the hare, the rabbit, the vole, the deer, and the Persian fallow deer in the Upper Galilee, and the snow vole on Mt. Hermon. The mammals of the warm area, usually found in the southern regions of our country, include: the jackal (that lives in packs close to settled areas, where their howls are heard at night), the wildcat (several species), the gazelle (in large numbers in Transjordan), the Arabic gazelle, the stag (few remaining on Mt. Carmel), the ibex (in large numbers, especially in the vicinity of the Dead Sea), the giraffe, chamois, antelope (on

Isaiah Press (1874–1955), geographer, scholar, and educator, wrote several travel books as well as the four-volume *Geographical-Historical Encyclopedia of the Land of Israel*, considered the first comprehensive geographical account in Hebrew.

the country's eastern and southern borders), the oryx (in the Negev desert), the sluggard, the mole, the stone-marten, the porcupine, the rat, the bat, Egyptian mongoose, the sow (usually found in the Jordan Valley and the secondary valleys), the wild donkey in East Hauran, the house mouse, the birch mouse, the lowlands mouse, the gerbil, the hedgehog-mouse, the fat sand rat, the jerboa (in the prairies and deserts, especially in Transjordan), and the dog. The Eretz-Israeli wolf resembles that of India, and the local hyena is not dangerous to man. […]

Birds
Local flying fowl include numerous birds, such as the cuckoo, which pass through at the beginning of winter and at its end, on their way to and from the warm lands. Some spend the winter in the country's warm areas (the Jordan Valley and Arnon Stream), where they hatch, such as the European nightingale. Song birds are scarce, but in some places their chirping is widely heard, especially in Transjordan and in the vicinity of the Arnon Stream and Wadi Sa'ir near Halhul, north of Hebron. The most common birds include: the sparrow (several species, including the pretty Dead Sea sparrow), the throstle (song thrush), the siskin (several species), the wren, the wagtail, the house sparrow, the bulbul (the Eretz-Israeli nightingale), the swallow, a hot climate bird, and the yellowhammer near the Dead Sea; the crow, the lark, the woodpecker, the kingfisher, the hoopoe, the nightjar. In the Jordan Forest across from Jericho there is also a unique genus of the hummingbird.

Also widespread are birds of prey, particularly the vulture, the black kite, and the black vulture (by the Dead Sea and the Litani River). Also the nightjar, the sparrow-hawk, the owl, and the Athene owl. Marsh and shrub birds abound in the country, specifically in the vicinity of Lake Huleh and in the Jezreel Valley, among them: the (white and black) stork, the crow, the flamingo, the osprey, the wild goose, the wild duck, the swan, the woodcock, the crane, the bustard (pelican), the ostrich sometimes comes from the Syrian-Arab desert to Transjordan. There is the poultry family, including the chicken, as well as the partridge (found abundantly throughout the country), the desert grouse (near the Dead Sea), the local quail (throughout all fields in the coastal area), and the partridge (forest grouse). The wild pigeon passes through the country in large flocks (especially in the Jezreel Valley).

Chicken raising in Eretz-Israel is still insubstantial, only in Gaza and Hebron are chickens grown in large quantities. Pigeons, turkeys, geese, and ducks are grown only in a few places of settlement.

Reptiles
Many reptiles are found on land and in water. Of snakes there are 33 species on land, including highly poisonous ones, such as the Egyptian cobra and a type of Indian viper (Daboia Xanthina). The venomous snakes usually live in the valleys and lowlands, many of them especially in the flat deserts of Jericho, and their venom kills those bitten within several hours. Many poisonous snakes also live in the country's waters, and only rarely come to shore.

Of the lizards there are 44 species. They live under rocks, in rock mounds, and in caves. A monotypic genus is the Stellagama (Stellagama stellio). It is dark colored, and its spine and tail are adjusted. Also belonging to the lizard family are the chameleon and the gecko. Small-sized examples of the African crocodile were found in Wadi az-Zarqa, south of Mt. Carmel. There are tortoises, large and small, as well as frogs in large numbers.

Insects

Among the insects one must note the scorpion that lives under rocks, and whose sting is deadly to humans. There are forty species of the grasshopper locally; most of them do not damage crops. Real damage is caused by the locust that sometimes comes westward in heavy swarms and spreads throughout the country, destroying all vegetation. Variously colored butterflies of different species add special grace to the meadows and flowering fields in the spring. Bees, wasps, spiders, flies, ants, and mosquitos are found in abundance.

The unique climate and variegated flora of Eretz-Israel make it suitable for beekeeping, in which many engage in the Judean hills, the coastal plain, and the Galilee. This industry is primitive among the *fellahs* (Arab peasants), but among the Jews and Germans, who have implemented European methods, and move the hives several times a year, to be near blooming flowers, it is much more profitable. They extract honey four times a year, 50 kg of each hive in total.

Fish

Eretz-Israel's waters are rich in fish. The finest fish are in the Mediterranean, along the country's coastline. In the Sea of Galilee, Lake Huleh, the Jordan River, and in all streams—forty-three species have been found. In the Sea of Galilee alone, which is very rich in fish, there are forty species.

Erotic Soil.

In the second half of the 19th century, Jewish settlers began coming to Palestine; young and idealistic, they arrived in Ottoman Palestine to till its land, establish agricultural settlements, and create a new Jewish identity—secular, active, and autonomous.

Immigration to Palestine was a part of the great emigration waves of the 19th century, during which many millions of people left Europe, and headed to the New World. The reasons for the mass migration were diverse, primarily demographic growth, economic crises, and famine. In the Jewish context, one must also add anti-Semitic persecution and restrictions imposed on occupation, property, mobility, and education acquisition. The majority of Jewish immigrants from Eastern Europe made their way to the United States; a minority was driven by the idealistic idea of Zionist nationalism.

The writings of these settlers indicate an extraordinary bond with the place in which they chose to settle, an affinity underlain by passion—desire for the land, the soil, its clods of earth and sands. The images of land cultivation are overtly erotic: nursing at the earth's bosom, piercing a virgin land, wetting the plowed furrows with nocturnal emission, inserting semen in a womb. The pioneering immigrant must submit to his ruling lady, and his desire is the realization of a thirsty land's yearning for a savior.

Abraham Shlonsky

Yield

[...]

You rhymed:
Our heart is a palace
the Holy of Holies
padded with tapestries and
  expensive gifts.
But I would not be ashamed:
If my heart were a barn
a stable
a sty
and every cattle would
  discharge its droppings
  and secretions in me.

For every heart is dear to
  me, with its cattle and its
  secretions.
Come, herd, and procreate
  with me!
From any full udder I shall
  drink milk
and with any warm dropping
  I shall fertilise my field.

[...]

Here

[...]

Lick, lick, oh summer-sun,
the corpse of my coarse land.
We shall draw from night-breasts,
for its soil,
dew-milk!

[...]

Like Glittering Light
Yehuda Yaari, 1937

> As the sun emerged from behind the mountains we pierced the soil with our plowshares. [...] Yes, there is something great about cutting through the ground with a plow! But there is something seventy-seven times greater about cutting through virgin land that no plow had touched for thousands of years! We felt that we were gathering in this soil's ancient shame, that we were betrothing with this plow the fields of the valley.

Yehuda Yaari (1900–1982) was a writer, playwright, and translator.

In Days of Vision and Siege
Shmuel Dayan, 1953

> We will soften it with blood and sweat, we will wet it with the dew of our youth and renew its youth, and it will remember us. We will renew that which flows with milk and honey—that which breeds giants—and heroes will rise among us and we will be redeemed.

Shmuel Dayan (1891–1968) immigrated to Palestine from Russia in 1908. A leader of the Labor Settlement Movement and a member of the Knesset in the first decade of the State of Israel.

On the Shores of the Sea of Galilee
R., member of the Labor and Defense Battalion in Migdal, 1921

The Kinneret sends its quiet waters into distant spaces. Giant mountains cast themselves around it like loyal brothers guarding their delicate and innocent sister. The waters of the lake give off softness and warmth, the mountains lofty simplicity. An infinitely deep blue sky stretches over them like a temple's majestic dome. And a hush of sacred awe pervades all. The blue, bright lake waters are silent, the mountains stand quietly as if deep in thought, dreaming of the transparent blue sky overhead. Sit here and relax, old wanderer, wash your dust-covered feet in the lake's living waters, sit and say not a word. Here your weary soul can rest, you can unite and meld with the majesty of creation, lose yourself in the concealing waves of stillness that reign all around. […]

And in shaking off your sleep […] rise up and approach the mountain and here there is something that will make your soul marvel. Listen to the pounding sound of hundreds of picks and hammers, and see blocks of stone rising in the air and rolling down, sparks flying, the mountain trembling, trembling here and there from the detonation of dynamite. And from within this great roar and clamor a great and vigorous singing like the breath of spring will reach your ear—this is the song of the smiths beating life from death, and this is their song, the song of war.

Portraying Progress.

By the 1930s Zionist organizations were obsessed not only with the actual colonization of the land, but also with propaganda, aimed at gaining support for the Jewish resettlement of Palestine. Among other things, they used aerial photography, both as a means for surveying for land development and as propaganda vis-à-vis the British limits on immigration. Such photographs were used for publication in newspapers and magazines in Europe and North America, and as a medium for display in international exhibitions. Their symbolism suggests spatial command and dominance, and they were often exhibited in a "before and after" setting, ascribing qualities of progress and plenitude to the colonizing project versus the Arab population's backwardness.

Aerial photographs by Zoltan Kluger, exhibited at the Jewish Palestine Pavilion, New York World's Fair, 1939 » original caption: *"A Study in Contrast – above: Typical Arab village; below: Typical Jewish settlement"*

NAHALAL

KFAR YEHEZKIEL

PLANNIN

Town Plannin[g]

CIVILIZATION
By HARRY LEVIN

NOWHERE does a span of ten miles provide greater contrasts in the techniques of the world's oldest activity, the making of human shelter, than along the broad sweep of Haifa-Acre Bay. Crusader buildings and the palaces of Ottoman pashas. From the height of Carmel austere houses reflecting the newest in modern architecture glimpse down on Bedouin goat-hair tents whose style was venerable in the days of Moses. Five [mil]es lie between the two, and five thousand years. [Tho]ugh not to the same extent in all parts of the land, [suc]h contrast in habitations is a keynote of Palestine. [T]o the old diversity the multiformity of post-War immigration brought new confusion. Because a Jew from [Sa]markand builds differently than one who comes from [Ne]w York, an anarchy of styles sprang up. Foreign [infl]uences were introduced, unrelated to either climatic [tra]ditions or the cultural temper of the land.

[W]ith the onrush of immigration calling for more and [mor]e housing, circumstances pressed ahead of plans. [Pub]lic opinion was deeply concerned over the housing [prob]lem but largely indifferent to the way it was being [sol]ved. Even the authorities all too frequently turned [a b]lind eye on infractions of minimum town-planning [reg]ulations concerning height and light, frontages and [bui]lt-on areas.

[I]n the rural sphere, where growth was less feverish, [lan]d space more ample, the situation was some[wh]at better. Most of the post-war settlements, more[ov]er, were established by a central agency, the Zionist [Or]ganization, which could—and did—adopt systematic [pla]nning of villages, and ensured its execution.

[T]he Valley of Jezreel, in 1921, was the first scene of [suc]cessful large-scale planning. The planner, Richard [Ka]ufmann, began with the building of a groundwork [of] such vital considerations as economic principles, [he]alth, security and communications. But in the struc[ture] reared on it the human factor was equally decisive. [Th]e new and composite Jewish peasant life in Palestine [is] different from peasant life in most other lands. The [vill]age must be different also; it must reflect the settler's [de]sire for contact and cooperation with his neighbors [an]d for a highly developed common cultural life.

[T]he village that emerged, Nahalal, has become the [sta]ndard type of the *moshav* (smallholder village). [La]id out in a perfect circle, its economic and social life [is f]ocused in the center. Here, in a park, stands the vil[lag]e hall, which is also the theatre; around it are ranged [a] school, hospital, cooperative stores and other com[mu]nal offices. Behind the ring of homesteads, in the [seg]ment of a greater circle concentric with the first, are [a] garden, vegetable patch, poultry-run and outhouses [of] each homestead. Beyond this again, like the spokes [of] an enormous wheel, stretch the actual farms.

[T]he farmhouses are small. Few have more than two [ro]oms, enclosed verandah, kitchen and bathroom. [Ea]ch has a garden, planted with palms, rose-bushes [an]d a variety of flowers. There is both privacy and [fle]xibility, as well as an air of rural peace.

[G]eva and Ein Harod, the first planned *kvutzoth*, fol[low]ed. The completely communal form of life here dic[tat]ed the structure of the village. The whole was built around a central axis, the backbone of the settlement, in the center of which was the farmyard. Farm buildings were completely separated from household buildings, but all were organically bound together. The dining hall, usually the social and cultural nerve-center of the *kvutza*, was set between the farmyard and the living quarters.

There are 233 Jewish agricultural villages in Palestine, 190 of them the product of the post-War years. Through the watchfulness of the Zionist authorities and of semi-public and private settlement and credit institutions, such as the Palestine Jewish Colonization Association, Palestine Economic Corporation and Rural and Suburban Settlement Company, almost all the newer villages are wholly or largely planned in advance. So in them, at least, natural dignity and human contentment have a solid material base.

In probably no other city in the world, proportionately, have such vast sums from charitable sources been spent on combating housing distress as in Jerusalem. But because these expenditures lacked expert guidance the slum problem has been intensified, the task of the town-planner rendered more difficult. In recent years a comprehensive town plan was adopted and provision made for a primary need, more open space. But civilized living in Jerusalem has much leeway to make up.

Nor are all the more recent buildings worthy of its natural beauty, dignity and associations. Yet many of the houses in the suburbs and a number of the public buildings are models of simple-lined beauty and dignity—qualities not difficult to attain by use of the magnificent pink and white stone that abounds in the nearby hills.

Tel Aviv, risen from the sand, is built principally of concrete and brick; and because of its phenomenal growth in under thirty years has more jerry-building and crudities than any other city in the country. But it is striving today toward a new urbanity, beginning to distinguish between dignity and gracelessness, between essentials and inessentials in comfort and decoration, and learning how best to fuse the essentials that remain.

Its vigorous municipal government ensures that new quarters exhibit better planning and more dignity than the old, and has itself evolved a number of ambitious town-planning schemes. Notable among these is a large new civic center that will contain not only the municipal building but also a theatre (already erected), a museum and a park, the whole encircled by wide boulevards and a central belt of trees. Another plan has been drawn up which may completely transform the neglected seashore. The scheme is to reclaim a long strip of land, 150 meters wide, from the sea and on it to provide an open space, a marine drive and promenade and an arcaded esplanade along which will stand hotels, a shopping center and places of entertainment. The cost will be $15,000,000. But in normal times that is not beyond either the enterprise or the capacity of Tel Aviv. On the fringe of Tel Aviv, just beyond Jaffa, is Kiriath Avoda—Labor Town—an example of what can be done by organized mutual aid. It is one of the twelve urban *(Continued on page 100)*

PAGE SEVENTY-ONE

Jew and Soil
REUNITED

Jewish National Fund, instrument of land redemption in Palestine: Its principles and achievements

By ISRAEL GOLDSTEIN

Before the coming of the first Jewish pionee[rs] Palestine wells and springs had been allow[ed to] dry up, the land had been denuded of trees, n[othing] prevented the sand dunes from encroaching. [and] malarial swamps flourished in that once f[ertile] country. To this desolation came the Chal[utzim.] They drained swamps, built roads, removed s[tones] and rocks from the good earth. They sowed [and] reaped, fought disease and hostile neighbors, e[stab]lished a new homeland for themselves and [their] children. In this work of redemption the Je[wish] National Fund was the public instrument.

4   SELF-EVIDENT proposition which is often forgotten is that there could never have arisen in Palestine a Jewish National Home [th]ere had not been, deep-rooted in the Jewish [peop]le, a hunger for land and for labor on the land. [No a]mount of propaganda and admonition can turn [reluc]tant city dwellers into successful farmers unless [a ge]nuine impulse toward a life on the soil can be [fann]ed into cooperation. If within the span of a gen[erati]on a hundred thousand Jews, the backbone of [the]homeland in Palestine, have found their per[sona]l destiny in agriculture, abandoning the shop, [the]market-place and the factory for the field and [the]plough, the explanation is that an inner, spir[itual] need was at work, much more potent than [exter]nal economic pressure.

Therefore the public instrument which is concerned with purchasing tracts of land in Palestine as the perpetual possession of the Jewish people, and with making them available for colonization, has aptly been named the Jewish National Fund. The original Hebrew name, *Keren Kayemeth le-Israel*, is even more descriptive: The Fund for the Endurance (or Maintenance) of Israel. When Zionism was a dream projected on the screen of the future, the emphasis on relationship to land gave the image its special character: Jews were to go to Palestine, but the Jewish settlement there was not to be a replica of the eternally landless Jewish communities of the exile. It was to be a normal, soil-bound, soil-nourished organism. In this alone could there be assurance of endurance or self-maintenance.

Following a Journey from Ramallah toward the Coastal Plain
Yosef Weitz, 1941

I passed through a significant part of northwestern Judea, back and forth, today, and saw: large, densely populated villages, surrounded by cultivated land: olive groves, figs and grape vines, sorghum fields and sesame, and fields of stubble. Indeed, there were also large areas of wilderness, still waiting for a cultivating hand, but will these suffice us? Will we be able to construct villages of our own scattered among their numerous existing villages, which will always outnumber ours? Can land there be purchased at all? Roads have facilitated development of the highlands and opened them to the big wide world; everything that grows from the land will be needed and required; there are hands available—why won't they develop it further, as they have heretofore? Could we not thus develop our nook? Again I heard within me that inner voice calling: "Clear this land," and then it shall be built, and our nation shall be built with it.

Yosef Weitz (1890–1972), known as the "Father of the Forests," played a major role in the forestation of Palestine-Israel in his capacity as director in the Jewish National Fund (KKL-JNF), which acquired many lands (ca. 250,000 acres) throughout the country. His writings are interspersed with scenic descriptions attesting to love of the land, alongside an orderly action plan for its Judaization.

Forest and Afforestation in Israel
Yosef Weitz, 1970

Indeed, our country has "nature": mountain and valley; desert and field; plain and rift; yellow sand and brown soil; perennial and seasonal streams; sunny days and rainy days; west winds and east winds, and all of them have fundamental appearances that have remained unchanged since time immemorial. This "nature," however, has a "garment," which is the landscape; and this landscape has been subject to multiple transformations, most inflicted by man. The landscape of our country as a geographical unit is multifarious in shades and sights, according to its changing political boundaries. The forested landscape of the Ephraim Mountains before their conquest by that tribe differed entirely from the scenery following their conquest and settlement by tribe members, when the forests were cleared and houses were erected in their stead, fields were plowed and vineyards planted. The battle between the desert and the field brings about scenic transformations following the desert's settling and vice versa. The country's landscape in the First Temple period clearly differed from its landscape during the Second Temple period, and especially toward its end. These clearly differ from the country's landscape after its occupation by the Arab Bedouin—the shepherds, who "destroyed the fences, disfigured the trees, and desecrated the land"; or from the landscape revealed to the Jews who returned to Zion in our time [...], which was nothing more than a landscape of desolation, the result of deliberate depravity and a product of thoughtless neglect. A landscape of desolation and destruction that not only should not be preserved, but should be replaced by another, by a landscape of culture and settlement.

Lamentation.

Memory Talked to Me and Walked Away
Salman Natour, 2014

Like the rings engraved in the olive trunk, the grooves adorning Abu Muhammad's face recount the chronicles of Palestine. The first groove stretches from his upper jaw to the tip of the eyebrow, attesting to the period of the Great Arab Revolt. It is reminiscent of the Syrian-African rift, which extends along the Dead Sea and the Jordan River. The second groove, which is cut short above the lower forehead, surrenders the year of dryness and drought. The third groove is the groove of banishment. It wiggles several millimeters above the drought groove, enfolding dozens of additional small wrinkles. But the most conspicuous of all is the groove of the Occupation. It extends above the chin, from the side of his left cheek to the side of his right cheek. Therefore, it would not be a figure of speech to say that Abu Muhammad's face has turned into a map of the history of Palestine. After all, Sheikh Abu Muhammad is like all other Palestinians.

Salman Natour (1949–2016), a writer, journalist, and playwright born in the Druze village of Dalyat el-Carmel, was editor of the culture section of the daily *Al-Ittihad*, among the founders of the Israeli-Palestinian Committee of Artists and Writers against the Occupation, and co-founder of the Arabic to Hebrew Translators Forum at the Van Leer Jerusalem Institute.

Netta Laufer, 25 ft, 2016; 35 cm, 2017 »

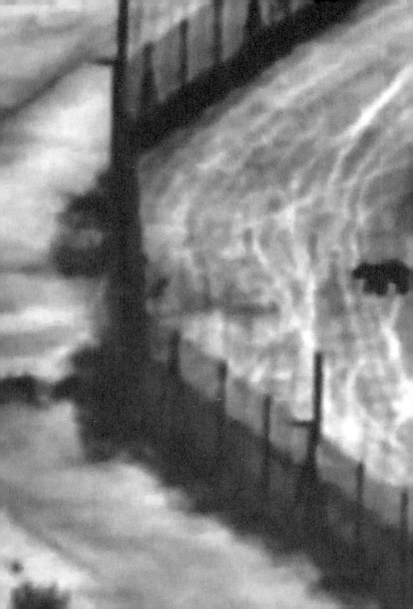

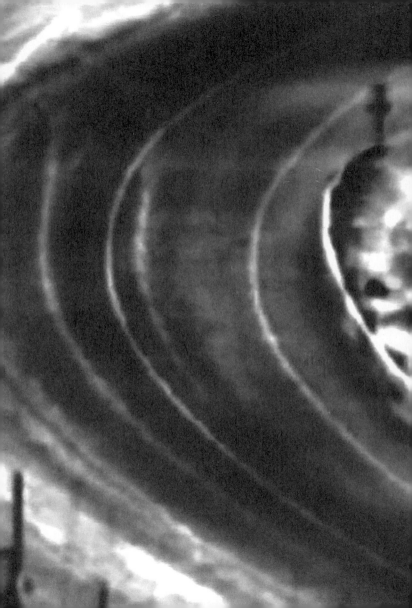

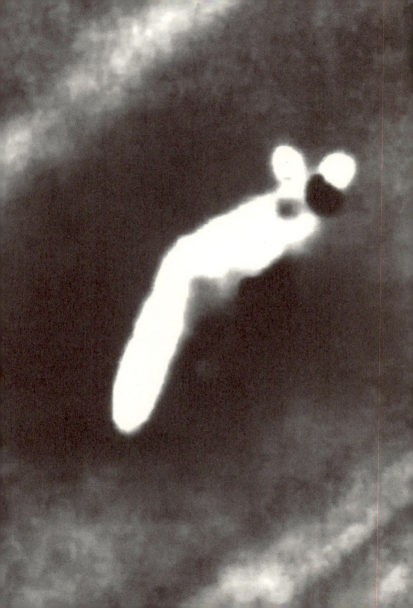

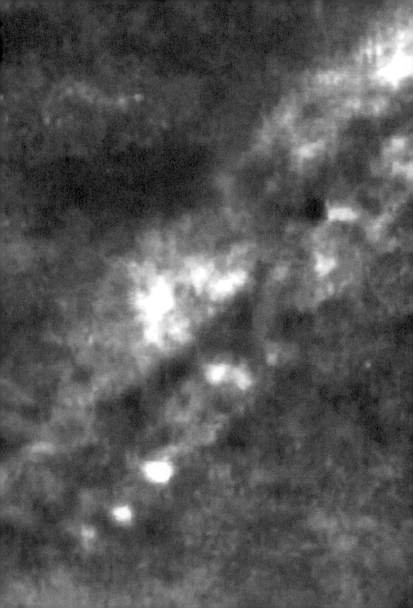

Sheikha Helawy

Stream

I'm not interested in the stream near my village that dies at the foothills of the Carmel Mountain

I'm not interested in the road that separated the shacks from the stream

I'm also not interested in the Jewish settlement behind the stream (I hated its lights glowing in the darkness)

I'm not interested in the measurement of the streamflow or in its name, which I never remembered

I am interested in remembering why I almost drowned in it

And why I didn't.

Milk and Honey
Chapter 2

The biblical phrase "a land flowing with milk and honey" appears many times in the Scriptures and has usually been interpreted as a metaphor for abundance. Many generations of Christians and Jews used it when they imagined the Holy Land. Yet, with the increasing European presence in Palestine, this metaphor became a powerful tool for demonstrating the gap between the imagined and the real, and exposed blindness to local forms of life, production of knowledge, and expertise.

According to this European understanding, this land of the Bible had prospered in ancient times, but had since decayed. This theme of decline was widely discussed and debated in European interpretations of the land. Furthermore, this debate regarding the land's ancient past encapsulated grander tensions of European colonialism in the Middle East. Adopting the Bible as a historical document, however, the European settlers believed that the land of Palestine was the land described in the Bible, and as such, it should literally be bountiful with honey and milk. For both Christian and Jewish settlers, a path to redeem the land from its perceived impoverished state emerged through tillage. Developing and improving agricultural practices in Palestine, therefore, reflected a desire to demonstrate the sacred potential of the land. To justify seizing control and transforming Palestine, the future had to look brighter than this past. To European settlers, Christians and Jews alike, the land, as part of this paradigm, should become extraordinarily plentiful, and its creatures—extremely productive.

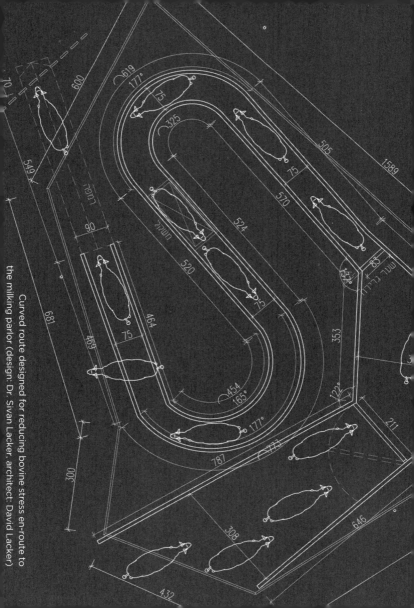

Curved route designed for reducing bovine stress en-route to the milking parlor (design: Dr. Sivan Lacker, architect: David Lacker)

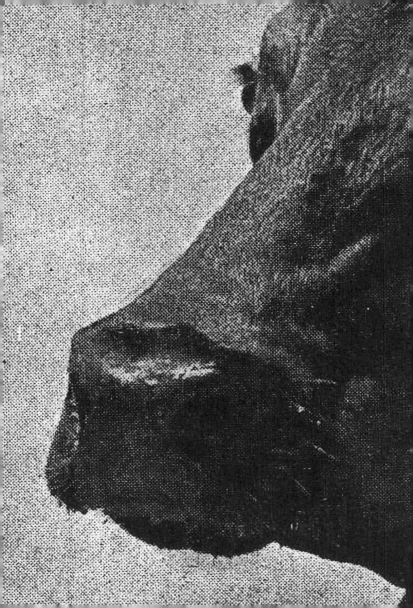

-A-
The Making of the Hebrew Cow

Veterinary Medicine in Eretz-Israel
Dr. Ami Neria, 2001

Cattle Breeds in Palestine in the Early 20th Century
According to the first estimate of livestock counts in Palestine carried out by the British Mandate authorities, there were approximately 108,500 heads of cattle here in 1920, of which 24,681 were dairy cows, most of them of the *baladi* breed, the majority of them owned by the Arab population.

The Baladi Cow: The Local Arab Cattle. The *baladi* cow can be found in most countries of the Mediterranean basin. Archaeological excavations indicate that these cattle have been here from biblical times, and likely have not changed much over the years. It is a small cow, brown or black colored with white spots, and its head is usually white. The breed has adapted to the special spatial conditions over the years, and has found its place in the primitive farm of the local Arab peasant (*fellah*). The weight of an adult cow ranges from 200 to 250 kg, and she yields between 400 and 700 liters of milk per year. Most of its food comes from grazing. The calving season is in January-February (one to two months after the start of the rainy season). In springtime the cows gain weight, keeping it through the summer, and losing weight in the fall and early winter. Itzhak Elazari-Volcani wrote about the *baladi* cow: "This breed is neither a milk nor a meat nor a work animal, but an ornamental beast that adds grace to the landscape's beauty. Its only virtue is that for generations it has

Dr. **Ami Neria** (b. 1929), a veterinarian and the author of a book about the history of veterinary medicine in Israel between 1917 and 1967.

toughened and withstands illness better than other breeds." This breed has apparently developed good resistance to regional diseases, especially tick fever. Cattle used to have thousands of ticks when young and became infected with disease, which at a young age passes relatively easily. Thus they would acquire immunity that usually lasted throughout their life.

The Damascene Cow. It is a near typical milk cow. Her body is narrow and her legs are high, the head is narrow and elongated, and so is the neck. The horns are undeveloped and sometimes degenerate. The hallmark of this breed is the developed nipple. The udder hangs like a sack, and the nipples are long and thin. Its color is reddish to dark brown. The adult cow weighs from 350 to 500 kg. The bull's weight may reach up to 700 kg. [...] Another positive feature is their ability to maintain a stable body temperature during the hot summer hours, compared to European dairy breeds. Its most important feature, however, is its productivity. In the Hebrew farm, in the 1920s, the Damascus cow reached a 2,500-liter milk yield per year with four percent fat. With improved feeding conditions, it reached up to 3,000 liters, and there were even a few cows that produced between 4,000 and 5,000 liters of milk annually.

The Beirut Cow. Her name probably came from being purchased mainly in the vicinity of the Lebanese capital. Her frame is stronger than that of the Damascus cow, and also broader, and it is shorter than the latter. It is usually light brown, its weight ranges from 250 to 300 kg, and its usual yield is 1,500 to 2,000 liters of milk per year. [...]

120 ‹ The Hebrew Cow ›

The German Cow. Settlers in the country (the Templars) developed and nurtured the cow industry for both dairy and meat products. [...] In 1910 they imported a red-and-white Ostfriesland bull to the country, which mated with the cows for two years and sired a number of good offspring, whereas in 1914 a black-and-white Frisian bull was imported; he was active for three years, and sired numerous offspring. This bull directly impregnated the local cows. [...] The term "German cow" indicates the place of breeding (the German colonies) rather than a specific breed. Of these cows, however, a fair number were purchased by the Jewish settlers.

The Buffalo (Jamus): The Black Cattle. In the first livestock count in Palestine conducted in 1921, 615 buffaloes were registered. Their actual number at that time is now estimated to be much greater. They didn't have much financial significance. They were raised in the marshlands of the Huleh Valley, near the shores of the Sea of Galilee, and in the lowlands near the marshes of Kebarah and Yarkon. Their milk yield was about 650 liters a year. The percentage of fat in their milk is higher than that of cow milk. Over the years, the buffaloes have been pushed out of the coastal plain, and remain only in the Huleh area.

Heifer at Ein Ganim, 1930 (photo: Yaacov Katznelson)

‹ The Hebrew Cow ›

Land Flowing with Milk. From the first quarter of the 20th century, the settlers and governing authorities alike insisted on positioning the dairy industry at the spearhead of the agricultural economy. These efforts translated into work in the fields of breeding and feeding, in an attempt to create an appropriate, bettered kind of cow. Crossing Middle-Eastern cows with European bulls gained prominence in the first half of the 20th century. The so-called "Hebrew Cow" emerged as a symbol of the success and challenges in settling the lands of the East. Dairy experts have continually taken pride in the milk yield and in milking technologies, and in recent years have named the Israeli cow a "world champion," as it produces an average of almost 12,000 liters of milk per year.

Milking facility, Kibbutz Tel Yosef, ca. 1925

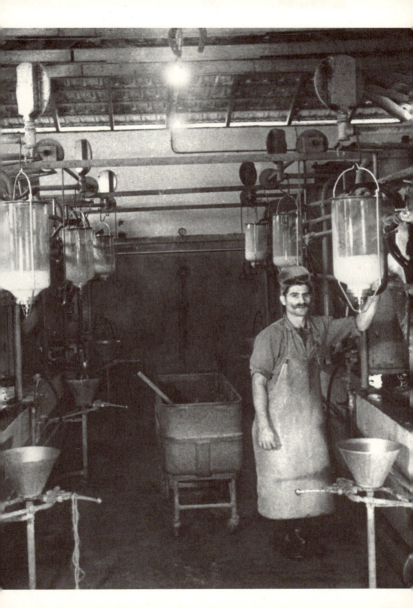

The Design of Agriculture in the Land (of Israel)
Itzhak Elazari-Volcani, 1937

"A land flowing with milk and honey" sounds like an exaggeration to many, whether because the people of the Orient spoke in hyperbole or because of the limited attainment of the desert wanderers. But the vision of today will become tomorrow's mundane reality. This small land is capable of supporting a million cows, rather than the 60,000 it does today. [...] What science achieves through research in decades, tradition has not reached in centuries.

Itzhak Elazari-Volcani (Wilkanski, 1880–1955), an agronomist, botanist, and writer, immigrated to Palestine in 1908, where he later established the Experimental Agricultural Station, and founded an institute for agricultural research, which remains the central institute of its kind to this day and is now named after him—the Volcani Center.

PUBLICATIONS of the PALESTINE ECONOMIC SOCIETY

THE DAIRY INDUSTRY
AS A BASIS FOR COLONISATION IN PALESTINE

by

I. Elazari-Volcani

P.Z.E. Agricultural Experiment Station, Division of Rural Economics

assisted by Dr. A. SUSSMANN

Tel-Aviv, September 1928.

Amanut Printing-Press, 68 Herzl Str. Tel-Aviv

Modernization and technological efficiency in the Hebrew dairy industry: Tnuva Dairy, Haifa, 1941; Agricultural School for Women, Nahalal, 1936 (photo: Zoltan Kluger)

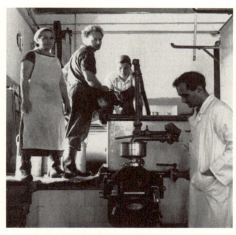

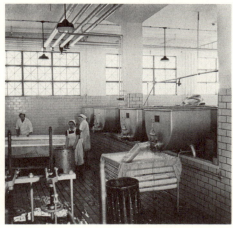

Tnuva Dairy, Degania, ca. 1930 (photo: Naftali Oppenheim)

128 ‹ The Hebrew Cow ›

As opposed to the European tradition, settlers' dairy cattle management focused on yield rather than looks, or as one expert noted admirably, "the exterior is lousy, but the yield is excellent." The emphasis on the efficacy of reproductive organs correlated with the ways in which cows in Palestine-Israel were photographed—that is, from behind and as a group (in order to show the reproductive organs), rather than individually and from the side, as was common in European cattle exhibitions.

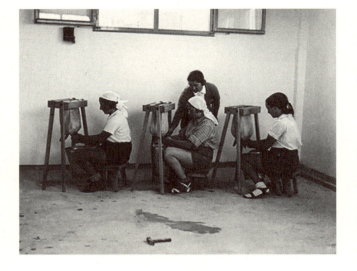

Young woman milking a cow, Kvutzat Kinneret, 1936 (photo: Israel Golan) ~ Milking training, Nahalal, 1936 (photo: Zoltan Kluger) ‹

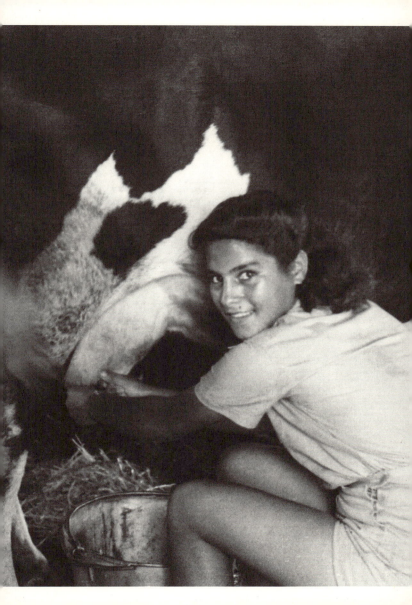

Cows photographed from behind:
Milking at Kibbutz Ginegar, 1930s

The development of the dairy industry is also a story of trial and error, struggle and failure, as cows and their owners dealt with the environmental challenges of heat, sand, scarcity of water and grazing areas, and finally, infertility. Annual pregnancies are crucial for cows to continue producing milk, making fertility a center of attention for the industry. The problem of infertility and miscarriages in cows has been widely discussed since the 1930s, layered by the realization that climate affects reproduction. Puzzlement over the relation between the local environment and the fertility of cows, and hence the production of milk, persisted, creating a need for novel ways to manage cows. Artificial insemination emerged as a solution to such problems. Many were skeptical, but with time, and with improving techniques, it finally replaced older methods of breeding. The "Hebrew Cow," whose creation was now made possible with the experienced hand of the human inseminator, never had to meet a bull again.

Insemination in action, Kibbutz Mizra, 1981 (photo: Zvi Marcus)

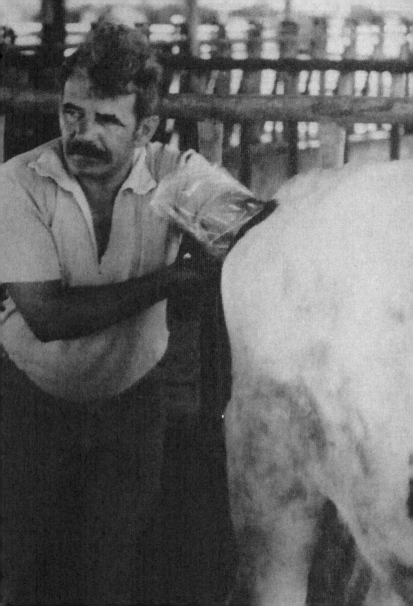

134 ‹The Hebrew Cow›

History of Dairy Farming in Israel
Uriel Levy, 1983

In a steaming tin-roofed cowshed, housing about six cows, stood the longing milkers. Three men marched in confidently from the bull pen. One carried a three-liter glass enema and a long tube in his hand; the other "held the hygiene": soap, Lysol, towel; and the third—just a curious onlooker. After removing the filth, washing their hands, and whispering—whispers which were possibly a swearing in, possibly a vent for the excitement—the rubber tube was inserted deep into the cow's vagina, and, at the order "release," the saline solution flowed along with the semen squeezed from a pinch of cotton, which had been taken from the vagina of the recently inseminated cow. The stream of enema liquid cleaned the cow's vagina, and burst out from the vulva lips, until the enema was empty. Was the cow impregnated? Three weeks later it was determined: No.

Uriel Levy (1908-1993) of the Israeli Cattle Breeders Association took a literary liberty in describing one of the first experiments with insemination carried out at the experimental agricultural station at Kibbutz Gvat, notwithstanding violent connotations.

All About Stavit: A Bovine Biography
Tamar Novick, 2019

Crowds of settlers in white shirts arrived in Kibbutz Kfar Giladi for the coronation. It was an autumn day in 1950, and Israeli flags flew high. The guests surrounded the ceremonial platform in anticipation of the local marvel—one dairy cow named Stavit (Heb. Autumnal) that won the title of "Champion of Champions." The participants, some 1,500 in number, came from all over the country, and some even came from Lebanon, the Netherlands, and Australia, to celebrate Stavit's impressive lifetime yield—100,000 liters of milk—as well as her fertility—15 calvings in 17 years (16 calves in total). At the end of the festive ceremony, which included a parade, speeches, and tying a gold-embroidered blue ribbon to the outstanding cow's aging body, the guests quenched their thirst with milk. The feted queen, on her part, "stood pensive in the middle of the green, quietly chewing her cud."

Following the festivities and their public resonance, Stavit became a celebrity. She starred in the press and became the choice subject of songs, quips, and visual documentation. In addition to a sculpture carved in her image, which was presented during the aforesaid ceremony at the kibbutz, her bovine body was presented in the press from diverse angles: in profile, as customary, to reveal her size; from behind, to show her milked udders; and even from the front—to show her facial features, as befitting a national heroine. Moreover, a special postmark was issued in honor of her championship, and a souvenir postcard bearing her picture was distributed among the guests. She reached old

Stavit, the cow from Kibbutz Kfar Giladi, ca. 1950

age—which is rather unusual in the case of livestock like her—and her death caused general mourning. As indicated by her story below, in her milk yields and fertility, Stavit symbolized the successes of the Jewish settling enterprise, since her udders overcame environmental obstacles and proved, time and again, that agricultural technologies can realize an ideology. […]

Stavit the Cross-bred Cow

Stavit was born on December 7, 1932 in Kibbutz Kfar Giladi to a Damascene cow named Esther Zmira (or, sometimes, Esther 1), and weighed 30 kg. Her father was a celebrated Dutch stud bull befittingly named Hercules. Both her parents were offspring of migrant stock imported to mandatory Palestine: Esther's mother came from the area of Damascus in the early 1920s, and Esther herself was born in the cowshed of Kibbutz Kfar Giladi in 1926; Hercules's Dutch mother came on a ship, carrying him in her womb, and so, the pure Dutch bull was also born in Palestine. Stavit was the outcome of Esther's third calving and the firstborn of Hercules who, over the years, became the father and grandfather of many "record-winning" cows—Stavit's sisters, daughters, nieces, and granddaughters.

Little is known about the lives and deaths of Esther and Hercules, but neither was exceptional to its time and setting. The dairy industry was developed among European settlers since the beginning of the 20th century, initially among the Christian Templars, and in the wake of World War I, by Jewish settlers with the encouragement of the mandatory government. Cowsheds soon became the basis of Jewish agricultural as part of the "mixed farming" economy promoted by experts in the agricultural experimentation stations. Dairy farming gradually evolved, and milch cows were imported from Damascus and Beirut, since they were more proliferous than the local cows referred to as *baladi* (Arab. local, native), which functioned not only as milk producers, but also, mainly, as draft animals. In contrast, the northern cows, nicknamed Damascene, were the result of many generations of breeding for milk production. Esther Zmira was such a Damascene dairy cow: the daughter of an imported, "migrant" Damascene cow that grew up in Palestine. […]

In the mid-1920s the deliveries of stud bulls from Europe, intended to improve the local herds, increased. A few bulls were imported from Germany at the end of the 19th century by Templar settlers, and the British government sent bulls from England and Ireland, which were placed in the government agricultural experimental farm in Acre, and were loaned to local residents to mate with their cows. Jewish settlers brought stud bulls mainly from the Netherlands, which was considered the world hub of milk yield expertise at the time. Hercules's mother probably came here as part of a transport of cows and bulls that arrived from Holland on December 27, 1924, along with Ephraim Shmaragd (1902–1976), a cattle expert who immigrated to Palestine after graduating agronomy studies in Utrecht. Upon arrival he settled in Kfar Giladi, and Hercules may have been born on that kibbutz, presumably in 1925.

Like her peers, Stavit was first generation offspring of a cross-breeding of an Eastern cow and a Western bull. The indigenous cows failed to yield sufficient milk, as the settlers desired, while European cows did not survive the immigration to Palestine and passed away soon after arrival in the cattle sheds. Cross-breeding was intended to combine the local species' sturdiness, its immunity to environmental difficulties and disease, with the milk production quality and fertility of the European breeds, to "spawn a settler, mixed, yielding cow." In the first years, experts recommended continuation of the cross-bred cow's cross-breeding with the local species to increase the survivability of the "mixed breed," arguing that the cross-breeding ideal was one third European and two-thirds local. In the late 1930s, however, with the escalation of the Arab Revolt, they changed their recommendation and determined that crossing of the cross-bred cows should be done, rather, with European bulls to promote the breed's yield. The new cross-breeding ideal was reversed, and now stood at one third local and two-thirds European. [...]

Not much is known about Stavit in her years as a heifer. In retrospect, her caregivers noted that in her young years she did not stand out in comparison to her peers, and was even somewhat sickly. Leafing through the Kfar Giladi herdbooks proves that she was a late bloomer, and became a part of the herd only at the age of 30 months, following her first pregnancy—late for a first calving; most of her shed mates calved and began yielding milk during the first 18 months of their lives. Since the first calving, in the spring of 1935, Stavit's fertility was consistent, although not all of her offspring lived long. Her firstborn was intended for the life of a dairy cow, but according to cowshed records, she soon "died of fever." The second heifer, born 11 months later, "was slaughtered due to signs of degeneration." All of her other heifers, save one that "died abruptly," grew to be milk cows, and were therefore named as follows: Mosaica, Stalingrada, Stavanit, Simona, and Smadar. Seven of her 15 pregnancies yielded males (and one yielded twins). Due to their inability to produce milk, they were sent from the cowshed to the slaughterhouse (one may presume), and hence were never named.

Stavit—Cowshed Member

The issue of naming was central to cowshed management. The larger the number of dairy cows in the settlers' cowshed became, and the greater the quantity of milk produced by each cow following the cross-breeding became, the greater the need became for a system of organization, management, and follow-up of the events in the cowshed. One system to identify the different cows and measure their relative success was an educated use of names. The names of the dairy cows and stud bulls—that gradually gave way to artificial insemination technologies—attest (with a certain degree of humor) to various aspects and views in the fields of politics (Stalingrada), Hebrew society (Smadar), productivity (Poriya, to be discussed below), nature or character (Haviva, Heb. amiable, also discussed below), as well as physical fitness and potency (Hercules). The naming of milk cows was based on an organizing principle—the name of each heifer of a dairy cow from the same shed would begin with the same letter as the name of the dynasty's great mother. Thus, for instance, the names of Stavit's daughters and granddaughters began with the Hebrew letter Samech (S).

The main technology that enabled the organization and monitoring of the events in the cowshed was the "herdbook." This system of documentation was adopted by the Jewish settlers' farms beginning in 1933, following the gathering of the Committee for the Establishment of the Herdbook in the Cattle Breeders Association of Israel. The […] book specifies all the measures that need to be taken—recording all details in a cow's life: data concerning her birth, parents, the food consumed daily, her milk yield (three times a day), and the percentage of fat in the milk. The book also includes data regarding the milk production of each individual cow and of the entire herd according to monthly and annual sections, and contains the details of all offspring of each cow and their destinies, as well as the names of the bulls and the dates of mating in which the dairy dynasty was expanded.

As artificial insemination developed and became established locally in the mid-20th century, cows and bulls were no longer housed near each other. Unlike the mating of a cow and a stud, the controlled mating of the cows is based on man-aided insemination, injecting bull semen into their bodies. The transition to artificial insemination led to a

רישום הפרטים ל"ספר האלופות"

לתעודת הרשמה מס' __1__ של הפרה __"סתרית"(פס)__

פרטי התנובה:

הערות	שם הוולד	ימי חליבה	% השומן	שומן ק"ג	חלב בתקופה ק"ג	תאריך ההמלטה	המלטה מס.
% השומן מחושב לפי הממוצע של כל התקופות	עגלה "סמהא"	266	3.34	126.4	5845	12.5.35	1
	" "	265	3.34	153.0	4581	15.6.36	2
	" נשחטה	317	3.34	167.9	5027	15.5.37	3
	עגל	371	3.25	221.1	6822	3.4.38	4
	"	321	3.50	233.7	6665	11.7.39	5
	"	347	3.40	256.4	7536	14.6.40	6
	"	278	3.59	221.8	6773	6.10.41	7
	סטלינגרדה	288	3.48	227.1	6574	10.9.42	8
	סחרינה	278	3.43	235.1	6865	22.9.43	9
	עגל	419	3.26	286.0	8807	5.9.44	10
	האומטם	274	3.24	227.9	7132	26.11.45	11
% השומן ממוצע משני הקדפות.	עגל	324	3.12	267.5	9023	4.11.46	12
	סיסרנה	310	3.26	275.7	8456	6.1.48	13
	עגלה-מתה	307	3.41	274.7	8050	25.1.49	14
תקופה לא גמורה.	ספדר	222	3.52	210.7	6346	13.2.50	15
							16
							17
	תקופות החליבה						
		15	4586	3.34	5399.9	101798	סיכום חלקי
							הסיכום הסופי
		15	310	3.34	227.8	6818	ממוצע חלקי
							הממוצע הסופי
							ממוצע ליום הונה
							ממוצע ליום חליבה

(חתימה) ____

1786—8.50—10x50x2

considerable reduction of the bull population, since one bull could produce many doses of semen to fertilize thousands of cows. The bulls were thus concentrated in one place, and insemination institutes were established which provided semen and insemination services to cows countrywide. Mating of cows and stud bulls became outdated. Stavit's sperm donors (whose actual contact with her is doubtful) were Lord, Hercules (her father!), Nimrod, Barak, Kokhav, May, Nadav, and Getter—all of them were pedigreed Dutch stud bulls. Finally, the herdbook also records the various diseases from which the cow suffered, and sometimes also the treatments she received, as well as the date and cause of her death.

Stavit's number in Kibbutz Kfar Giladi's herdbook was 59. Her page contains comprehensive details about her life, and it is the major source for the nonpublic aspects of her biography—what may be regarded as her private or everyday life. Stavit began producing milk with the birth of her first heifer on May 12, 1935. During her first milking period (between the first time she gave birth and the last months of her second pregnancy) she was milked 255 days and yielded 3,845 liters of milk with 3.34% fat on average. The percentage of fat in her milk remained constant throughout her milking years, and is similar to the general average in Jewish dairy farms in the first decades following the establishment of the State, and even until the present. The formulation of intensive milking routines—three times a day—in Mediterranean climate conditions, led to a relatively low fat percentage compared with the European ideal, which was over 4%. The cattle experts regarded profuse milk as the major goal in the development of the Jewish settlement and as the best way to indicate the land's prosperity. Therefore they were willing to compromise for a low percentage of fat; in other words, they valued quantity over quality. The extensive use of the herdbook attests to the importance of quantity, since it is dedicated wholly to gathering, documenting, and comparing milk quantities and offspring over time for each individual cow and between different cows from different cowsheds. [...]

Stavit's milk yield grew consistently each year. In her third year in the cowshed (1938) she produced 4,764 liters of milk; in the fourth—5,114 liters, in the fifth—6,060 liters, in the ninth—7,407 liters, and in the twelfth—her peak year—she produced 8,823 liters of milk. Even in her more mature years Stavit was consistent in production, although it gradually reduced, until she was removed from the cowshed. In 1938 [...] she contracted the foot-and-mouth disease which threatened many farms in the late 1930s and continued to worry cattle growers over the years. She apparently was healed, as she stayed on in the cowshed and continued to produce milk systematically for more than a decade after that.

Not all the cows survived so many years in the cowshed, whether due to decrease in their milk yield or due to various physical ailments and diseases. In addition to Stavit's three daughters, that were slaughtered or died at a very young age, at least one more daughter also died during her mother's lifetime: Stalingrada (no. 242 in the herdbook), that produced milk for approximately four years, and died at the age of six from a "foreign object" in her body. Her most successful daughter, Stavanit (no. 272 in the herdbook) survived nearly 11 years in the kibbutz cowshed, but in 1954 she was "slaughtered due to sterility (a cervical infection)." Stavanit ended up in the slaughterhouse—"280 kg of meat," as noted at the bottom of her respective page.

Before becoming a chunk of meat, Stavanit earned public and professional recognition for her efforts. During her lifetime she produced 53,166 liters of milk, and was thus introduced into the "champion" milk cow club—cows that passed the 50,000-liter milk yield mark in their lifetime, an exceptional quantity in the time of Stavit and her daughters. [...] Milk yield such as Stavit's led to the creation of a new record category—"Champion of Champions"—which marked her as a legendary success within the excellence club, making her a public figure.

Celebrity
Stavit was not the first beast to gain public fame. The achievements of dairy cows were already measured and celebrated in the first years of Jewish dairy farming. In 1937, for instance, Zkufa (Heb. upright) from Kvutzat Kinneret, Haviva of Ein Harod, and Poriya of Geva won annual awards for milk yield and fat percentages. [...] Measuring cow achievements and milk yield competitions relied on a long tradition of cattle and livestock contests in Europe and the United States. Unlike the European and American instances, however, the local competitions focused on measuring milk production, rather than on the animal's physique or the percentage of fat in her milk. This is yet another proof of the ideal of plenty promoted by the settlement project, since quantity was more important than quality. Such spectacles served the Zionist enterprise: the outstanding cows on which the coronation ceremonies centered, were a mooing proof that technological manipulations overcame environmental and political obstacles. Stavit's crowning as "Champion of Champions" did more than that: it attested to the correspondence between the land and its settlers, since the results of that encounter, namely Stavit and her

milk yield, were extraordinary by world standards; this may well have been the origin of the "startup nation's" belief in exceptionalism.

Stavit's story became public in the beginning of summer 1950, many weeks before the coronation took place. Already in the early stages, her biography and the exceptional nature of her cumulating achievements were emphasized. Among others, she was described as the "queen of the cowshed" and a "cow of valor." "With her profuse milk," the daily *Davar* read in July, Stavit "exceeded the yield of all dairy cows in our country and in the Near East." Not only did she break the regional record, the same article noted, but she even scored a "world record" of lifetime yield surpassing 100,000 liters, a record which she shared with nine other dairy cows: the Russian Uputnica, an English cow, and seven American cows. It was Stavit's exceptional achievements that made her a public figure and justified the grand crowning event celebrated on the kibbutz.

Following a series of welcomes by the heads of the agricultural organizations and a reading of Stavit's chronicles to the large crowd, she was crowned "Champion of Champions" in the late morning hours of October 12, 1950. Her body was decorated with a blue ribbon, and her head was crowned with a laurel wreath. The guests received (or purchased, according to some accounts) a souvenir postcard bearing her picture, and a special postmark issued in her honor was announced. The ceremony culminated with a parade of the dynasty of excellence, including Stavit's surviving, successful daughters and granddaughters, one by one, and their accomplishments and lineage were made public (alongside other champion-milk cows: Naama, Elinoar, Kokhevet, Favia, Pkuda, and Elsa; 26 cows in all).

147

התאחדות מגדלי בקר בישראל

ספר העדר
תעודת אלופה
מס' 151

שם הפרה סתרית	מספר ספר 0
נולדה 7.12.1932	גזע ג×ד דור 1
המטפח	כפר גלעדי
בעל הפרה	כפר גלעדי
יצאה	סיבת היציאה

התאחדות מגדלי בקר בישראל

20 DEC 1964

חתימה   חותמת   תאריך

Stavit's champion certificate, Israeli Cattle Breeders' Association, 1964

The event received broad and diversified coverage: reports in the press, interviews, poems, jokes, and photos. A humorous play was staged, and at least one short film produced. Most of the coverage focused on the coronation itself; two articles were described as interviews with Stavit, going to lengths to delve into her inner soul. One, headlined "100,000 Liters of Milk from One Udder!: An interview with Stavit of Kfar Giladi and her grooms," highlighted her stardom, commencing as follows:

When an enlarged delegation of the IDF mouthpiece Bamahane knocked on the doors of Kfar Giladi's champion cowshed one hot Galilean afternoon to interview the distinguished Mrs. Stavit, both parties were in for a big surprise. We, who are infants in cow matters, were surprised by the modesty and humility with which this lauded young cow welcomed us, whose udders had become famed nationwide; she, on her part, turned wondering, tired eyes at the camera flash, the likes of which she had never encountered before, a sarcastic smile spilling over her aristocratic head—"another pest has come to disturb my peace."

[...] In the weeks following the ceremony Stavit became a social and political boxing ring. One writer of a letter to the daily Davar, who identified herself as "vegetarian," claimed that the state should reward Stavit and her fellow prolific dairy cows by not sending them to the slaughterhouse at the end of their lives:

Considering the great benefits we enjoyed from the proliferous commodity vital in rearing our children—the young generation, who are the kingpin of our nation—and as reward for their contribution to our economy, Stavit and her peers should be granted a more worthwhile prize than the champion's crown: that in their post-fertile days, when their udders shrink and can no longer produce such abundance of milk as in their youth, the aged cows will not end up in the slaughterhouse.

[...] Renowned Israeli poet Natan Alterman, in his poem "A Picture of the Cow Stavit," published in three versions over the years, likewise used Stavit to voice political criticism. Between the lines he expressed wonder at her public appearance and discussed the power of propaganda. [...]

The sense of surprise (whether sincere or not) that accompanied the public appearance of an individual that is a cow was congruent with the exceptional nature of that individual's accomplishments. At the same time, that same emphasized anomaly was, to a large extent, antithetical to the featured body itself, which was a rather ordinary one. In most of the depictions and various pictures of her published over the years, what stands out is the lack of uniqueness of that productive body, and most conspicuous is its old age. In early August 1950, it was reported that "Stavit has been the queen of Kfar Giladi's cowshed for many years. She stands upright in compartment no. 2." While "her figure is fine, her black skin is shiny, and she has all her teeth," "her hair has turned gray. She still has an appetite and is in good spirits." The ordinariness of her body was fundamental since Stavit symbolized, most of all, the scope of the entire dairy farm economy successes and its technological aspects: "A superb cow is like a state-of-the-art machine," one of her caregivers noted after her death. Stavit manifested dualities and contradictions to varying extents, being both ordinary and exceptional, a living body and a machine.

Stavit's uniqueness was also manifested in her depictions. Farm animals were customarily photographed in groups rather than individually. Most milk cows—the sophisticated

‹ The Hebrew Cow ›

milk-production machines—were depicted from behind to present the reproductive and milking organs. Some especially outstanding cows (such as the upright cow) and several stud-bulls were photographed alone and in profile, so that their physique was fully displayed. Stavit alone was photographed from the side and from the rear, and she is probably the only cow also depicted from the front in a manner which identifies her face. She is also the only cow to have a sculpture created in her image, and a postal cancellation issued. Her group photos were not in the company of other milk cows, but in the company of humans—three of the kibbutz dairymen who milked her. Under the photograph of this foursome appeared a one-line caption reading: "left to right: Stavit, Israel, Gershon, Haim—one champion and her three grooms."

About a year after she gained fame, it became known that unlike her peers, who were taken out of the cowshed when their milk yield declined, Stavit was allowed to age. By virtue of her exceptional achievements, and perhaps due to her celebrity status, the kibbutz decided to "reward her" and built a "retirement home" for her: a one-cow shed equipped with the necessary services and surrounded by a yard. Cowshed data indicate that she was officially removed from the milk cow group on July 15, 1952 due to the unusual reason of "old age," and lived as a non-productive creature for at least another six

Stavit and her caretakers; original caption: "From left to right: Stavit, Israel, Gershon, Haim—One champion and three grooms"

months until quitting the world. As befitting a star and a national heroine, her death at the end of January 1953 was followed by obituaries in the front pages of the labor movement newspapers. "Stavit passed away" and "Stavit is gone"—the headlines announced, and the articles reported: "Stavit—the queen of cows, who earned fame for her world record milk yield, passed away in Kibbutz Kfar Giladi. Stavit contracted a severe leg and stomach disease, and since she could not be cured, the doctors decided to end her suffering by slaughter. Stavit was 19 years old, and produced 107,971 kg of milk during her lifetime. She gave birth 15 times." The whereabouts of her burial place are unknown, possibly nonexistent.

Stavit's death notice, 1953

"**Stavit is Dead**; Stavit—the queen of cows, famed for achieving a world record in milk supply, 'passed away' in Kfar Giladi. Stavit contracted a severe stomach and leg disease, and since she couldn't be cured, the doctors decided to 'redeem her from pain by slaughter.' Stavit was 19 years old, and produced 107,971 kg of milk during her lifetime. She gave birth 15 times."

152 ‹ The Hebrew Cow ›

Transporting cows, 1960s

Living Together. Since the agricultural revolution more than ten thousand years ago, humans have lived in cohabitation with farm animals. For the most part, the animals were housed on the ground floor, which was often sunk into the ground, and humans lived above them. In the early Yishuv years, many of the settlers adopted this form of co-habitation, and lived with their animals under the same roof.

The Land of Israel: A Journal of Travels in Palestine
Henry Baker Tristram, 1863–64

> The houses, excepting the very poorest, seem all alike. Each has a courtyard, with a high wall, for the goats, camels, firewood, and bees. At the end of the yard stands the mud-built house, with a single door opening into its one room. A pillar and two arches run across it, and support the flat roof. The door opens into the stable portion, of which I have spoken before, where horses and camels are standing before the manger of dried mud. Stepping up from this, the visitor finds himself at once in the simple dwelling-room of the family. A large matting of flattened rush generally covers one half […].

Kibbutz Gan Shmuel's cowshed, 1920s

Cowshed Typologies. The early Zionists championed the concept of cooperative settlements. The new farm typologies were structured to produce the highest yields of milk, with specific attention to experimenting with cowshed design.

The Moshav, one of the two major Zionist types of cooperative settlements, was based on small, family-run, mixed-farming parcels, which were equal in size. Each family parcel maintained a close relation between the family's housing unit and that of the animal sheds.

The Kibbutz, the second major agrarian typology developed in the 1920s, espoused communal living in all facets of life. Since the settlers shared ownership of the settlement, spatial design did not necessitate parcelization. This enabled the complete zoning and consolidation of the "productive" areas, separating them from housing and other communal living facilities. Though socialist in its ideology, the typology of the kibbutz enabled the consolidation and design of large cowsheds and the benefit of economy of scale, leading to the ultimate Taylorized form of dairy production. To this day, several kibbutzim boast some of the largest cowsheds in the world.

The Moshav Farm
Emmanuel Yalan, 1959

A family farm is typified by the closeness of the residences to the "industrial" plant. Any solution that regards this as a flaw that should be avoided as much as possible, or endeavors to arbitrarily separate the residential and industrial spaces, will miss the mark. The integration of technical and spiritual functions must find its expression in physical integration. Both living conditions and pace of work should be reflected in the plan.

Emmanuel Yalan (1903–1981) was an Israeli architect and a professor at the Technion–Israel Institute of Technology, Haifa

158 ‹ The Hebrew Cow ›

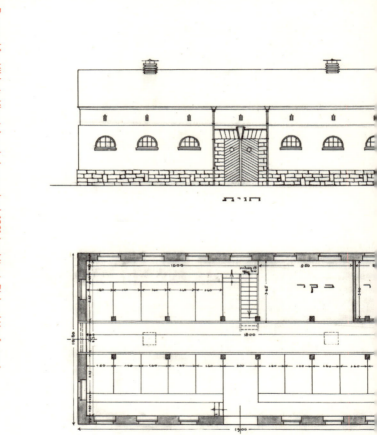

Proposal for Kibbutz Kiryat Anavim's cowshed, 1921 (architect: Richard Kaufmann)

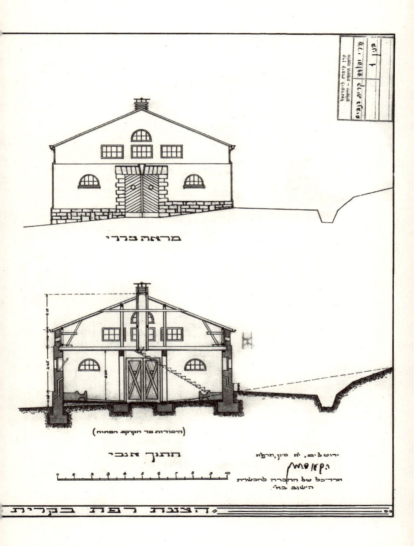

Cows in the shed, Kibbutz Kiryat Anavim, 1938 (photo: Zoltan Kluger)

162 ‹ The Hebrew Cow ›

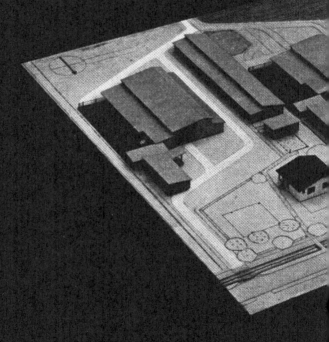

Model for farmyard organization, 1959 (architect: Emmanuel Yalan)

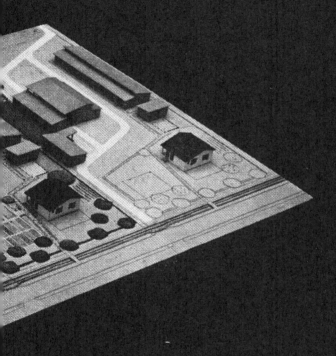

163

164 ‹ The Hebrew Cow ›

Zoometry. Architectural modernism has witnessed attempts to base design on efficiency in relation to the human body. Finding meaning in body measurement has a long social-Darwinian history, with notorious fields of study such as phrenology and craniometry. Borrowing from these traditions, cowshed design incorporated zoometry—the science of measuring animals' body parts and movements, along with studies of morphology and behavior. Efficiency of motion and ergonomic design of the living areas, as well as the ability to monitor physical metrics, became essential for farm planners, since the cow was not only the "worker," but the "factory" of production itself.

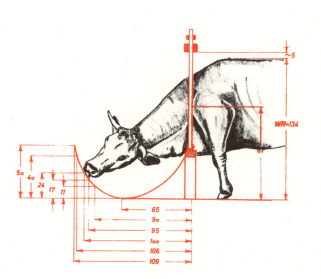

Zoometric drawings (from: Shalom Scherer, Zoometry, 1976) »

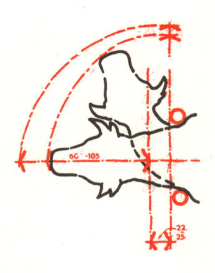
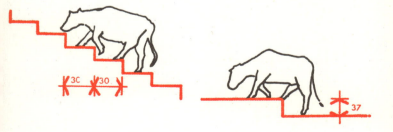

166 ‹ The Hebrew Cow ›

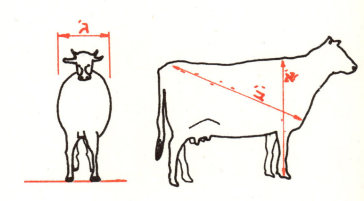

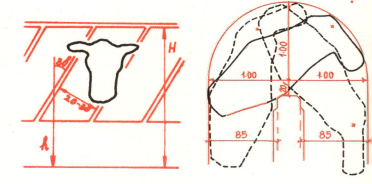

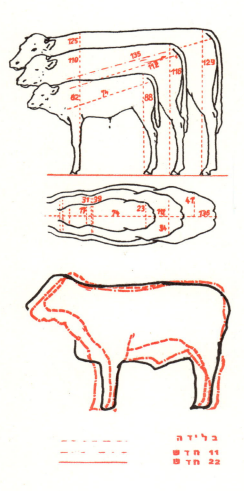

168 ‹ The Hebrew Cow ›

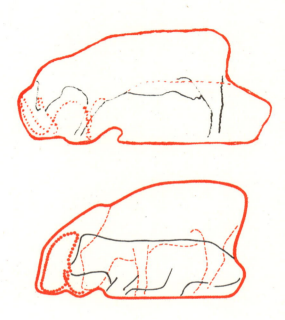

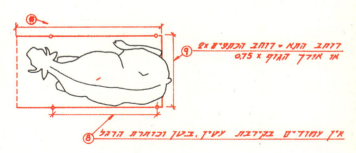

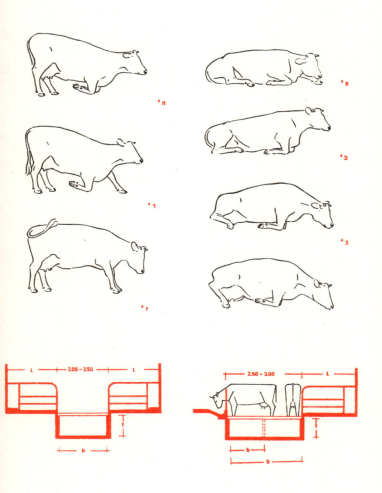

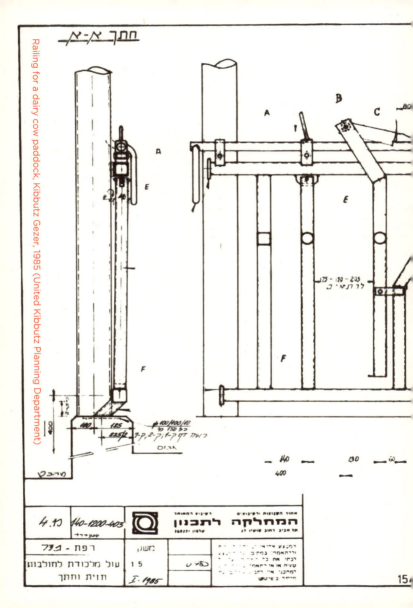

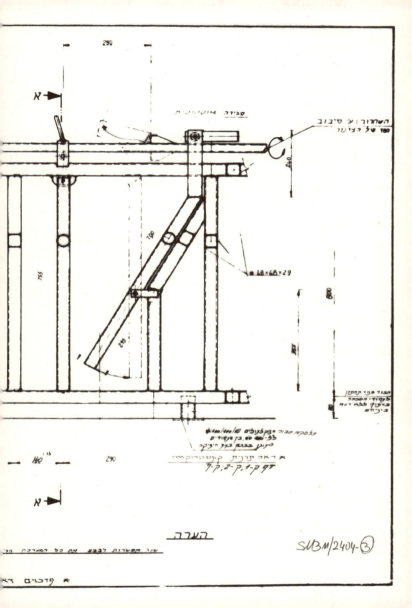

Home.

The cow spends most of her day lying in the shed's bedding area. The elongated roofs slope and shade a floor which is part concrete, partly unpaved. The shed is divided into three sections that extend all its length: the feeder at the center, flanked by areas designated for cows on either side; here they eat and drink and rest. Most of the time they stand by the food trough, their heads sticking through the bars, and eat. Food and water are served regularly, and they eat and drink at will. They never go out to pasture.

The cows are led to the milking parlor three times a day. The parlor is two-storied: a ground level and another level underground. The cows wait in the holding pen, where they are sprinkled with a gentle spray of water that cools their bodies as fans blow on them. They enter the parlor in turn, one by one. There are thirteen milking posts on each side of the hall, and each cow goes to her regular position; she already knows the way. The parlor employee connects the suction tubes to the udders, and the milking takes a few minutes. The milk flows through tubes to the basement floor, undergoes initial filtering, is transported to a stainless steel container for cooling, and from there to another container standing in the yard waiting for the truck. The Israeli cow produces approximately 12,000 liters a year on average.

The cowshed provides optimal living conditions for maximum milk production. Any physical inconvenience results in a decline in productivity, which is the measure by which cow welfare is assessed. Creating favorable conditions requires monitoring and studying the body: food, dimensions, movement ability and ways of restricting movement. Every aspect is examined and taken care of: food and nutrients are available throughout the day, body temperature is monitored, and a massage device to rub against is installed on the far end of the shed. Manure is shoveled into the spill containment pallet, or spread out on the ground.

Cows suffer from heat. The optimum temperature for them is much lower than the average Israeli temperature, which stands at 21°C and climbs above 30°C on summer days. To this end, electric ventilation systems, a system of skylights that open on hot days, water droplet spraying systems, and large circular fans that fill the cowshed with a monotonous growl, were installed. Architecturally, the cowshed is a climatic project, and is designed as a system of shading and ventilation.

Milk output is determined by the hormonal condition of the dairy cow. Maximum output means chain pregnancies. The first calving is set for two years, and each pregnancy lasts nine months. In the two months after the calving, milk yield is at its peak. Three months later, another insemination will take place, which will lead to another pregnancy. An average dairy cow in Israel goes through three or four pregnancy and milking cycles in her lifetime, each about a year-long. When her fertility declines, milk yield also drops, and she is taken out of the milking circle and sent to the slaughterhouse.

The calf is separated from its mother upon birth. To prevent disease, the calves are raised separately—each calf in its own little cage. Once grown, the male calves are sold for slaughter. The heifers are moved to the common cowshed, and after their first pregnancy, they are integrated in the milking routine.

Mating is performed via artificial insemination and fertilization procedures. The semen is collected from the males on the stud farm, or bought overseas. Its monetary value is determined by genetic quality, and is intended to ensure yielding, calm, healthy cows.

Design of the cowshed relies on careful study of the cow's body. The planners make extensive use of architectural tools for measurement, drafting, and data processing, whereby the different parts of the shed are designed: fencing systems, feeding areas, conductance routes, milking posts.

The cow is subjected to constant monitoring. To monitor their physical condition and make sure that they are not in distress, which could lead to decrease in milk output, a sensor is attached to the cow's neck or leg, which monitors variable data, such as activity, milk quality, and pedometer readings, from which conclusions can be drawn about the cow's fertility and health. The cowshed has become an orderly system, which includes continuous data mining and real-time treatment adjustment.

The cowshed is a hybrid facility: a home and factory in one—a multi-armed system made of tin, concrete, stainless steel, sensors, udders, stomachs, and hooves. The building, the sensor, the body, and the machine have merged into one.

The cowshed is a kingdom of matter. Milk is associated with cleanliness, health, and purity; the manure requires treatment, disposal, and disinfection; concrete, mud, tin, and body excretions are pitted against the shiny stainless steel containers, which hold the yield of this biological plant. At times, the sky, the clouds, and the cypress trees are reflected in them, as if it were an Anish Kapoor sculpture.

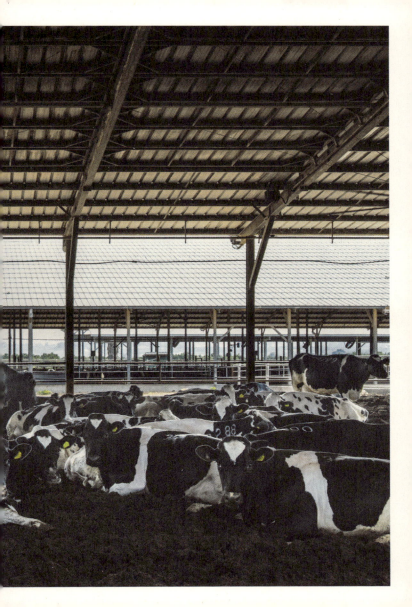

-B-
Bee Colonization

‹ Bee Colonization ›

Wild Bees. Palestine-Israel is exceptional in its bee variety. Of a total of 1,600 species of bees known to man, more than 1,100 live in Israel-Palestine. Most wild bees do not live in complex social structures, and none produce honey for humans to enjoy. They have other environmental roles to play. As in many other parts of the world, however, and as a result of the use of pesticides, ever-growing limitation in open spaces, and the domination of honeybees, utilized for honey production and pollination services, wild bees are endangered.

Beekeeping. Honeybees have gradually come to dominate the local landscape. Archaeological evidence show that organized beekeeping began in this area of the world, dating back to the 8th century BCE. Beekeepers in Palestine-Israel pride themselves in continuing a centuries-old practice, and many have referred to the frequent mentions of honey in the Old Testament by way of naturalizing their practice. This tendency to use the Bible as a manual for agricultural work proved especially fruitful at the turn of the 20th century, as new forms of beekeeping and changing bodies of bees aided in demonstrating that honey could indeed flow in this land.

"Palestine Honey Production": Report by the US Consul in Jerusalem, 2 November 1921

PALESTINE HONEY PRODUCTION.

American Consul.

Jerusalem, Palestine.   November 2, 1921.

Whether or not Palestine has literally become a land
flowing with milk and honey is now being tested in a prac-
tical and commercial manner. The possibilities for the
commercial production of honey have received most definite
attention, and interest therein has recently and rapidly
increased.

Commercial Honey Industry Dates From 1882.

There has always been at least a minor production of
honey in Palestine for local consumption. This production
has been by use of the primitive native hives made of baked
earthenware jars with the orifice reduced to a small size
for the ingress and egress of the bees and an opening out
into the wide part of the jar to permit removal of the honey-
comb. These hives are stationary and owing to the fact that
flowers bloom but for a few weeks in any given locality in
Palestine the honey-making season is necessarily brief unless portable hives are used. In 1882 the first use of
portable hives in bee culture was made by an Alsatian family
settled in this country. An attempt was made to interest
the natives in these modern methods but without any appreci-
able success. In later years, however, the Jewish immigrants
to Palestine who came here to found agricultural colonies
have taken up honey production on modern lines. Quite
recently the efforts of the Jewish colonists in this industry

The Land of Israel: A Journal of Travels in Palestine
Henry Baker Tristram, 1863–64

Olive-oil, goats'-hair, and tobacco, seem to be the principal produce of the district; the latter being exported in some quantities, by way of Acre, to Egypt. Bee-keeping, also, is not an unimportant item of industry, and every house possesses a pile of bee-hives in its yard. Though similar in its habits, the hive-bee of Palestine is a different species from our own. We never found *Apis mellifica L.*, our domestic species, in the country, though it very possibly occurs in the North; but the common Holy Land insect, *Apis ligustica*, is amazingly abundant, both in hives, in rocks, and in old hollow trees. It is smaller than our bee, with brighter yellow bands on the thorax and abdomen, which is rather wasp-like in shape, and with very long antennae. In its habits, and especially in the immense population of neuters in each community, and in the drones cast forth in autumn, it resembles the other species. Its sting, also, is quite as sharp. The hives are very simple, consisting of large tubes of sun-dried mud, like gas-pipes, about four feet long, and closed with mud at each end, leaving only an aperture in the centre, large enough for two or three bees to pass at a time. The insect appears to frequent both doors equally. The tubes are laid in rows horizontally, and piled in a pyramid. I counted one of these colonies, consisting of seventy-eight tubes, each a distinct hive. Coolness being the great object, the whole is thickly plastered over with mud, and covered with boughs, while a branch is stuck in the ground at each end, to assist the bees in alighting. At first, we took these singular structures for ovens or hen-houses. The barbarous practice of destroying the swarms for their honey is unknown. When the hives are full, the clay is removed from the ends of the pipes, and the honey extracted with an iron hook; those pieces of comb which contain young bees being carefully replaced, and the hives then closed up again. Everywhere during our journey, we found honey was always to be purchased; and it is used by the natives for many culinary purposes, and especially for the preparation of sweet cakes. It has the delicate aromatic flavour of the thyme-scented honey of Hybla or Hymettus.

But however extensive are the bee colonies of the villages, the number of wild bees of the same species is far greater. The innumerable fissures and clefts of the limestone rocks, which everywhere flank the valleys, afford in their recesses secure shelter for any number of swarms; and many of the Bedouin, particularly in the wilderness of Judaea, obtain their subsistence by bee-hunting, bringing into Jerusalem jars of that wild honey on which John the Baptist fed in the wilderness; and which Jonathan had long before unwittingly tasted, when the comb had dropped on the ground from the hollow tree in which it was suspended. The visitor to the Wady Kurn, when he sees the busy multitudes of bees about its cliffs, cannot but recall to mind the promise, "With honey out of the stony rock would I have satisfied thee." There is no epithet of the land of promise more true to the letter, even to the present day, than this, that it was "a land flowing with milk and honey."

Man and the Bee: Beekeeping in Israel
Israel Robert Blum, 1951

I was granted an opportunity to observe these natural builders while moving hundreds of families from the Arab pots into state-of-the-art beehives. One must note that the lives of bees in the Eastern pots are almost natural. Other than the introduction of the swarm into the pot and the extraction of honey therefrom, all the work orders in the pot are left to the bees themselves. To move a family from such an Arab pot to a modern hive, one must shatter the pot, which is usually made of clay, whereupon the construction of the honeycombs is made visible. […]

I received these pots from different climatic environments, from the Shfela (the Judean foothills), the Golan Heights, and the Upper Galilee.

Israel Robert Blum (1898–1979), a Czech Jew who immigrated to Palestine in 1924 and became a successful apiarist and a leading figure in the Jewish beekeeping community, wrote the first Hebrew book on beekeeping.

Sun-dried mud beehive
(illustration: Israel Robert Blum)

Indigenous beekeeping: clay beehives heaped under a stone arch, late 19th century

Palestinian clay apiary, Bethlehem, late 19th century (photo: Ludwig Armbruster)

‹ Bee Colonization ›

Movement in the Hive. These were turbulent days for bees and their keepers. The moveable-frame beehive, which gained prominence across the globe in the Age of Empire, arrived in Palestine in 1880. Gradually replacing the commonly used fixed clay hive, the success of this technology was sweeping: while fixed clay hives limited honey production to local, seasonal swarming, the movable-frame beehive enabled a year-long production cycle, which was not limited to local flora. The new mobility of hives and bees aided in increasing honey production, and provided a justification for intervening in native forms of living.

David Ardi, head beekeeper of Kibbutz Gan Shmuel, transferring bees from clay beehives to moveable frame hives, 1928

‹ Bee Colonization ›

En Kamel, læsset med Bi-Stader.

Camel transferring moveable frame beehives, ca. 1890

From Cedar to Hyssop: A Study in the Folklore of Plants in Palestine
Grace M. Crowfoot and Louise Baldensperger, 1932

When the time came to take the bees from the orange blossom of Jaffa to the thymy uplands they bound the hives on a camel and proposed to travel by night while the bees were asleep.

As the European settlement project began taking hold in Palestine, moveable-frame beekeeping was explicitly promoted, professionalized, and standardized. The use of the static clay hive was discouraged, and its practitioners delegitimized.

Field of moveable frame hives, Jaffa, 1890

Press Notice by the British Mandate Government
25 July 1933

> Modern methods are essential, and the Government Department will be glad, at its various beekeeping stations, and especially at Acre, to give all enquirers the fullest information and advice on the subject, to sell bees of good stock [...] and in particular to give practical demonstrations of the superiority of movable comb-hives over mud-hives. With mud-hives, the bees have often to be killed before the honey can be extracted, and then it is full of impurities; with movable comb-hives, the honey can be removed in its purity without harming the comb or the brood, and natural swarming can be controlled and the number of colonies of bees increased as the beekeeper wishes.

A beehive cut open near Mount Carmel, 1890 (photo: Ludwig Armbruster)

The New Bee. Transforming honey production required more than just changing the hives. The bodies of bees themselves had to be transformed and perfected to fit the new way of managing the land and the ultimate production of honey. Experiments with breeding began with mixing neighboring Egyptian and Syrian breeds, resulting in the so-called *Apis mellifica var. Terra Santa*—the Holy Land bee. Ultimately, as in many other places, the Italian bee won over.

The Beekeeper from Kibbutz Gan Shmuel Apiary, 1987

Hadera was a major beekeeping center back then: an area flowing with bee-attracting "honey plants," citrus orchards, and Eucalyptus forests, marshes teeming with wetland plants as well as dune vegetation on the sand dunes. After acquaintance with the apiary in Hadera—the Gan Shmuel apiary was like a dream to me. Order, cleanliness, and beauty reigned supreme: a tidy warehouse, equipped with an electric honey extractor, a motorized knife, equipment for raising queen bees and an incubator, a wax processing apparatus.

The apiary stood at the heart of the kibbutz. The beehives were colored in white and silver, placed on cinder bricks in straight lines, numbered and arranged amidst flowering bushes. I was so impressed, that I must have decided there and then to tie my life to beekeeping, as in Gan Shmuel.

David Ardi was not a man of many words: he spoke little, but he was a man of bees. As a young beekeeper,

David Ardi (1902–1986) was a beekeeper in Kibbutz Gan Shmuel Apiary and served as Head of the Beekeeping Department in the Israel Ministry of Agriculture, 1948–1967.

thrilled at the sight of the beautiful, secret-holding apiary, I wanted to know. I asked many questions—and the answers were brief. David told me: "You want to know about bees? Open a hive, observe, watch, and learn." David was proud of his beekeeping achievements, his work methods, the quiet bees, and the ample honey yield.

* * *

The Gan Shmuel apiary was the best equipped in the country at the time, and the most professional. Its yield was 54 kg of honey on average per hive. David Ardi always had ideas and initiatives for advancement. The hive was populated by the local (Syrian) bee, which was aggressive and difficult to handle. David ordered queen bees from Italy, and began bettering the species, replacing a local bee with an Italian bee. The process was implemented by adding an Italian queen-bee to a local swarm. Over a period of two to four years we succeeded in replacing the local bee with an Italian bee. David was the first in the country to engage in this field.

Beehives of Kibbutz Yagur against the backdrop of Mount Carmel, 1930s

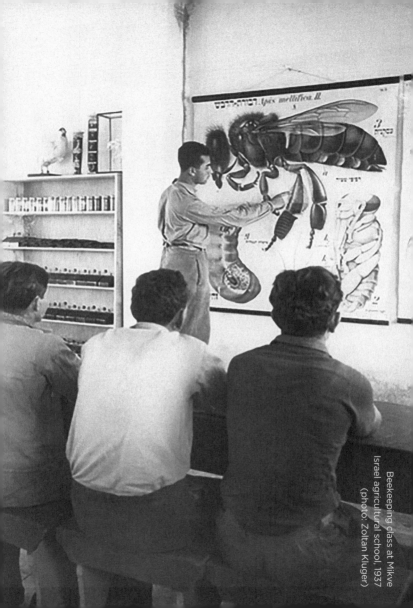

Beekeeping class at Mikve Israel agricultural school, 1937 (photo: Zoltan Kluger)

208 ‹ Bee Colonization ›

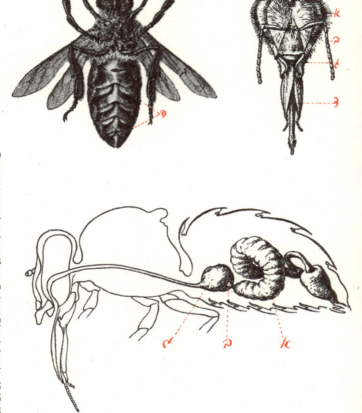

Bee anatomy drawings (from Robert Blum's books, 1943, 1951)

209

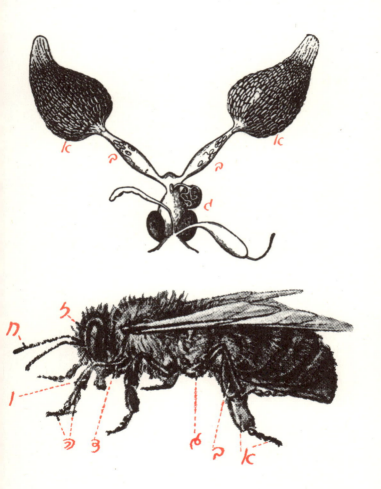

Beeswax queen cells, Kibbutz Beit HaShita, 1960s (photo: Azaria Alon)

Man and the Bee: Beekeeping in Israel
Israel Robert Blum, 1951

> Our goal is propagation, and not mere propagation. While our native bees have not let us down, this year an act is to be performed which might let them down. We shall see to it that the new families will be of a foreign breed, an Italian breed, and we shall also replace the existing families with that species. Not out of love of the foreign, but because the Italian bee is quieter, stings less, easier to handle, and provides at least 50% more honey.
>
> What is the secret blessing of the Italian bee? It may sound like a paradox, but I shall venture to say nonetheless: the local bee may produce an equal amount of honey as its Italian counterpart, but it gives less to the beekeeper. [...]
>
> But I will admit, the Italian bee has one great disadvantage. It is far more delicate than the native bee, it is not as quarrelsome as its compatriots, and this weakness is most discernible in their struggle against wasps. It is thus our obligation to release them of that war duty. Its weakness, however, is also its great advantage: it is much gentler to the keeper.

« Queen-breeding technologies, Kibbutz Gan Shmuel, 1936 »

214 ‹ Bee Colonization ›

Man and the Bee: Beekeeping in Israel
Israel Robert Blum, 1951

> Man's knowledge enables him today to delve deeper into the lives of bees; more than with any other domesticated animal, he decrees their fate and dominates most of their activities. But, relying on our knowledge, we can do a great thing, something our forefathers were unable to do: aided by the ongoing work of experts, man can now eliminate, or at least weaken, certain qualities of the bee which are undesirable, such as its irate, stingy nature, while concurrently developing desirable qualities.

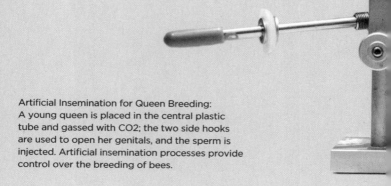

Artificial Insemination for Queen Breeding: A young queen is placed in the central plastic tube and gassed with CO_2; the two side hooks are used to open her genitals, and the sperm is injected. Artificial insemination processes provide control over the breeding of bees.

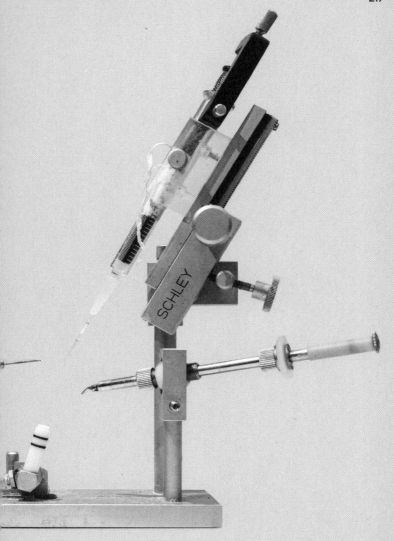

217

-C-
Scapegoat

Goats at Wadi Fara, 1920

Shepherd and goats near Kibbutz Alonim, 1936 (photo: Zoltan Kluger)

Goats were the greatest population of domesticated animals in Palestine and the main producers of milk for hundreds of years.

Europeans visiting and settling in Palestine were surprised and disappointed to find it, by their standards, desolate and barren, and saw the planting of trees a central tool in improving, developing, and controlling the land. British officials in Mandatory Palestine therefore implemented a policy of afforestation, which was considered a major way to utilize land resources throughout the entirety of the British Empire.

Foresters, the main agents executing such ideas about afforestation, demonstrated their fondness for trees. There were, however, other creatures that loved them even more: particularly, the herd of local goats who had a great appetite for young pine trees, and complete disregard for newly established borders.

Goats grazing and nibbling trees near Sheikh Abreik, 1938 (photo: Zoltan Kluger)

According to the British paradigm, goats and other grazing animals damaged nature in Palestine, and sabotaged the potential rescue of the land from its current desolate state. This translated into a multilayered course of action that included classification, enumeration, vaccination regimes, and plans for controlling and limiting the movement and numbers of goats in Palestine. As goat overgrazing was seen as a major factor in the deforestation of the region, grazing regulations and restrictions developed rapidly.

The tools for controlling and handling goats included systematic registration of all goats by owner and village, taxation, penalties, vaccination schemes, and standardization through the licensing of shepherds.

Disinfecting and vaccinating goats in a field near Jaffa, supervised by British officials, 1934 (photo: Zvi Oron)

From the 1930s onward, it became clear that Palestinian peasantry was also perceived as threatening and unstable to government rule, just as the grazing goats were considered threatening and unstable to the land. Harmful in similar ways, these two—Palestinian peasantry and Palestinian goats— therefore came to be seen as a threat to the stability of the land and the state.

The Arab, The Goat and the Camel: "Destroyers of the Desert,"
Palestinian Post, 11 October 1934

Major C.S. Jarvis Bay, who has been Governor of Sinai for 12 years, stated in a lecture before the Royal Central Asian Society in London recently, that the Arab and the goat were responsible for desert wastes. He agreed that it was a misnomer to describe the Arab as the "Son of the Desert." He was really the "Father of the Desert."

"By failing to repair the ordinary wear and tear caused by the weather," said Major Jarvis, "and wantonly destroying everything for which they could find no immediate use, the Arabs have allowed the country to slip back to the desolation from which a more virile race reclaimed it before their coming. In this campaign of destruction, the Arab has been assisted loyally by his two animals—the camel and the goat— both of which are vandals and Philistines of the first water."

"Leader in the Mighty Wickedness": Major Jarvis referred to the Old Testament description of the goat as an evil beast— "a leader in mighty wickedness." He held the goat and his companion in crime, the camel, responsible for the "invasion

of sand that has spread all over Northern Sinai." By eating out the heart of every living plant, he said, they had removed all the binding material provided by Nature for the stabilization of sand, and the accumulation of rapidly-moving dunes was the result.

Arab's Joy: Major Jarvis said that litigation was the Arab's one joy in life. "He may have other hobbies, but I have never discovered them," he said, "and my experience is that lawsuits occupy his mind to the exclusion of all else. This is due partly to the fact that litigation costs nothing in the Sinai Arab Courts. If an Arab ever has to settle an English solicitor's bill of costs for a trifling action, it would knock litigation on the head as far as he was concerned for all time."

232 ‹ Scapegoat ›

"Types of goats": left: a local, black goat;
right: Damascene brown goat (from manuals for
Hebrew settlers on management of sheep and goats)

233

The 1948 War sparked a dramatic reduction in the number of Palestinian goats, decreasing estimates of 750,000 in 1946 to 100,000 four years later (not unlike estimates regarding decreasing Palestinian population). Despite these reduced goat numbers, government officials in the now-called State of Israel quickly expanded formal attempts to control and eliminate them: in 1950, the Israeli government passed what is considered to be its first environmental law, the Plant Protection Law, later known as the Black Goat Law. In essence, its goal was to systematically reduce the number of black goats in the country.

Plant Protection (Damage by Goats) Law—1950

*Passed by the Knesset on the 27th Av, 5710 (10th August, 1950).
The Bill and an Explanatory Note were published in Hatza'ot Chok no. 47
of the 4th Tammuz, 5710 (19th June, 1950) p. 183 [Hebrew].*

1. In this Law— **Interpretation**

"grazing" includes permission to graze, causing to graze and the driving of goats otherwise than on a public way, and the verb "to graze" and all its derivatives shall be construed accordingly;

"inspector" means a person whom the Minister of Agriculture has appointed to be an inspector for the purpose of this Law;

"permitted rate" means—

(a) in respect of the period from the day of the coming into force of this Law to the 26th Sivan, 5711 (30th June, 1951)— one goat per twenty dunams of unirrigated land or one goat per five dunams of irrigated land;

(b) in respect of the period from the 27th Sivan, 5711 (1st July, 1951) onwards—one goat per forty dunams of unirrigated land or one goat per ten dunams of irrigated land.

Keeping of goats

2. A person shall not keep or graze goats save within the confines of the land occupied by him and at the permitted rate; provided that it shall be lawful to drive goats over any land to a place of grazing permitted under this section if the owner of the land has consented thereto.

Prohibited grazing

3. Notwithstanding anything in section 2 or in the Forests Ordinance, a person shall not graze goats—

(a) in a forest reserve or a closed forest area within the meaning of the Forests Ordinance;

(b) in any other area which the Minister of Agriculture, by declaration published in Reshumot, has declared to be an area in which the grazing of goats is prohibited.

Permit to keep and graze goats

4. The Minister of Agriculture, or a person authorised by him in that behalf, may permit in writing the keeping and grazing of goats on conditions to be prescribed in the permit.

Domestic goats

5. Notwithstanding anything in sections 2 and 3, it is lawful to keep goats of a number exceeding the permitted rate within the confines of the yard adjoining the house of their owner if they are shut up or tied up and fed within such confines; the Minister of Agriculture, or a person authorised by him in that behalf, may permit in writing the grazing of the said goats in certain seasons of the year even outside the confines of the said yard, but within the confines of the land occupied by their owner.

Power to enter

6. An inspector may, at any time, enter the confines of any land, other than a house or a yard, and carry out an inspection therein, if he suspects that any of the provisions of this Law is contravened therein.

Power to seize

7. (a) Where the inspector notices that the number of goats on any land exceeds the permitted rate in respect of either grazing or keeping, or where he notices a goat grazing contrary to the provisions of this Law, he may seize goats up to the number in

excess of the permitted rate, or the goat grazing contrary to the provisions of this Law, as the case may be, and sell them or it at the price which shall be prescribed by a person appointed in that behalf by the Minister of Agriculture by appointment published in Rashumot.

(b) At the time of the seizure, the inspector shall give the person keeping the goats a receipt for the goats seized.

Offences and penalties

8. **(a)** A person contravening any of the provisions of section 2 or 3, or a condition imposed under section 4, shall be liable to imprisonment for a term not exceeding six months or to a fine not exceeding one hundred and fifty pounds or to both such penalties.

(b) Where a person whose goats have been seized under section 7 is convicted of an offence under subsection (a), the Court shall order that the whole or a part of the price of the said goats shall be paid to the owner of the goats or shall be confiscated; in the event that the goats have not been sold under section 7, the price shall be determined by the Court.

(c) A court shall not consider a criminal action for an offence under subsection (a) filed against a person whose goats have been seized under section 7 unless the suit is filed within three months from the day on which the goats were seized.

Payment for value

9. Where goats have been seized under section 7, and a criminal action for an offence under section 8 (a) has not been filed against their owner within three months from the day on which they were seized, their value shall be paid to their owner.

(b) The owner of the goats may claim their value in the magistrate's court in whose area of jurisdiction they were seized.

(c) A court shall not consider a claim under subsection (b) unless —

(1) a criminal action for an offence under section 8 (a) has not been filed against the owner of the goats within three months from the day on which the goats were seized under section. 7; or

(2) a criminal action as aforesaid has been filed against the owner of the goats, but, he has not been convicted.

(d) A court shall not consider a claim under subsection (b) unless it is filed within one year from the day on which the goats were seized under section 7.

Implementation and regulations

10. The Minister of Agriculture is charged with the implementation of this Law and may make regulations as to any matter relating to such implementation, including regulations regulating the registration of goats and regulating the keeping and feeding of goats under section 5.

Commencement

11. This law shall come into force on the 23rd Tevet, 5711 (1st January, 1951).

David Ben-Gurion *Prime Minister*	**Dov Joseph** *Minister of Agriculture*	**Yosef Sprinzak** *Chairman of the Knesset Acting President of the State*

Black goats, 1948 (photo: Beno Rothenberg)

240 ‹ Scapegoat ›

Thumbprint signatures of goat owners from the village of Sakhnin, on a petition to the government of Israel protesting the Goat Damage Law, 28 December 1952

Summary of Goat Herds in the Arab Villages for the 1949–50 Season: The table concentrates the numbers of sheep and cattle heads in the Arab villages of the young State of Israel, divided into regions. This page refers to the Western Galilee and lists the localities in alphabetical order and according to the following columns: Grain field area / Rocky terrain / Total wild grazing terraces / No. of goats / No. of sheep / No. of cows and bulls / Total cattle / Total goats to eliminate / No. of sheep for rehabilitation / No. of cows for rehabilitation. The number of goats counted in each village is equal to the number of goats to be eliminated.

סיכום עדרי העיזים בכפרים הערבים לעונה 1949/50

מס׳ פרות לשקם	מס׳ כבשים לשקם	מס׳ עזים לחסל	סה"כ מקנה	מס׳ פרות שוריים	מס׳ כבשים	מס׳ עזים	סה"כ אדמות מרעה בד׳	שטח שרטים בד׳	שטח גדולי שדה בד׳	ש ם ה כ פ ר
										גליל מערבי
15	175	504	789	191	94	504	9597	2697	6900	1. אבו סנאן
50	440	1378	1874	388	118	1378	26686	12686	14000	2. עראבה
50	485	1471	2052	350	231	1471	11157	4857	6300	3. גוליס
40	365	1130	1243	113		1130	5038	4118	920	4. ג׳ת
25	250	754	1006	252		754	12369	7269	5100	5. דיר-חנה
13	100	334	522	173	15	334	7916	5666	2250	". דיר-אסעד
75	500	1744	2077	329	4	1744	25751	18901	6850	7. ירקה
95	500	1945	2192	247		1945	11810	10000	1810	8. ינוח
25	200	651	711	60		651	3565	135	3430	9. כאוכב
15	175	501	823	251	71	501	7276	3676	3600	10. כבול
47	300	1074	1240	166		1074	6697	4847	1850	11. כפר-סומיע
24	175	589	831	242		589	13715	9465	4250	12. מגדל-כרום
76	500	1768	2145	325	52	1768	18371	14621	3750	13. מעליה
20	200	697	1162	465		697	30119	19319	10800	14. מוג׳הר
18	150	485	856	232	139	485	12901	9951	2950	15. נחף
95	500	1944	2837	838	55	1944	53386	37024	16362	16. סכנין
13	150	430	648	106	112	430	1874		1874	17. סג׳ור
60	75	756	1139	383		756	22780	18280	4500	18. פסוטה
125	500	2235	2927	560	132	2235	29145	14345	14800	19. תרבה
10	150	394	749	287	68	394	13640	5140	8500	20. עילבון
14		141	226	28	57	141	370		370	21. תרשיחא
905	5890	20925	28059	5986	1148	20925	324163	202997	121166	ס ה " כ
										גליל עליון מזרחי
170	850	3394	3512	118		3394	21732	15591	6141	22. בית גן
30	195	689	1065	294	82	689	6650	4340	2310	23. ג׳יש
50	250	1033	1426	233	160	1033	15344	11294	4050	24. חורפיש
45	250	941	1157	143	73	941	8403	5403	3000	25. פקיעין
20	100	414	580	165	1	414	13547	12257	1290	26. רמה
10	35	168	747	205	168	374	2616	560	2056	27. ריחניה
325	1670	6845	8487	1158	484	6845	68292	49445	18847	ס ה " כ

The new state of Israel continued the British mandate afforestation project, turning tree planting into a national mission led by the Israeli government and executed by the Jewish National Fund (JNF/KKL). This went hand in hand with further restrictions on goat keeping and grazing.

Address to the Second Knesset's Opening Session
Prime Minister David Ben-Gurion, 1949

> We must plant hundreds of thousands of trees on an area of five million dunams (half a million hectares), a quarter of the country's total area. We must dress all the slopes and mountains in trees, all the hills and rocky ground unfit for cultivation, the sand dunes of the coastal plain, the Negev drylands east and south of Beer Sheva, meaning—the entire land of Edom and the Arava all the way to Eilat. We must also plant for security reasons, along all the borders, along all the roads, trails, and paths, around civilian as well as military buildings and installations. […] We would betray one of the state's two major goals—making the wilderness bloom—if we settle only for the needs of the hour and for work whose return is in the short run, and fail to undertake projects in this day and age which will be enjoyed by future generations. We are a nascent state repairing the wrongs inflicted for centuries, corruption to both the people and the land. To this end, we must recruit all the professional strengths we have in this country. […] Over time, we must reach a planting rate of half a million dunams (50,000 hectares) per year.

Balfour Forest near Kibbutz Ginegar during planting, 1946 (photo: Zoltan Kluger)

244 ‹ Scapegoat ›

The Israeli afforestation project on Mount Carmel, 1967

The fight against the black goat subsided over the years, but regained momentum in the 1970s. Following the 1967 War, herders from the newly conquered West Bank and Golan Heights were able to cross over to Israeli territory and extend their grazing territories. In essence, the West Bank came not only with a large Palestinian population, but also with a sizable population of hungry goats.

Regulations implemented by the Agriculture Ministry in the 1970s. Measures signed by the Minister of Agriculture in accordance with the Black Goat Law further restricted grazing territories in the late 1970s, and ordered confiscation of goats caught grazing in restricted zones.

Black Goats Crossed the Green Line and Annexed Pastures and Woodland
Maariv, 6 June 1974

"They cause heavy economic and ecological damage. They have grown in number tremendously since the Six-Day War, and are raised on territories within the Green Line since pastures in Judea and Samaria have been depleted."

עזים שחורות פלשו ל,קו הירו[ק]
וסיפחו שטחי מרעה וחורש

גורמות נזק כלכלי ואקולוגי כבד ★ התרבו במספר מדהים נ
מלחמת ששת הימים וגידולן נשען על השטחים שבתחום ",
הירוק" משום שמקורות המרעה ביהודה ושומרון כבר מדולד[ל]

מאת יוסף וקסמן

מבת העיזים השחורית, ששמן מעיר על צבען, מהריפה והנדהת. ריבויין, בעיקר מאז מלחמת ששת הימים, גדל באלפי אחוזים, והנזק הכלכלי וה־אקולוגי, שהן גורמות הוא כפר.

לא מכבר החלט להקים ועדה בין משרדית לבדיקת הבעיה, ובראשה יעמוד נציב משרד החקלאות.

העיזים השחורות משמידות שטחי חורש, ורועי העיזים מבצלים בחורשים על־ברות עצים ושריפתם, כדי להקל על תנועת העיזים וליצור שטחי מרעה גדולים וטובים יותר. העיזים השחורות גורמות נזק חמור לשטחי מרעה טבעיים. ואף מביאות עליהם כלי' בשל שימוש מופרז.

עד מלחמת ששת הימים מספרן בארץ היה אפסי. אחרי המלחמה חדרו העיזים השחורות בכמויות עצומות לתחומ ,,הקו הירוק". ואילו רועי העיזים ,,סיפחו" שטחי מרעה טבעיים וחורש מאזורי ,,הקו הירוק" הפנוי לשדרות מרעה לעיזים השחורות מיהודה ושומרון.

כפי שמתברר משיחות עם בני היישוטים, שהם מטפחי העיזים השחורות, אין שחוץ מאזורן של עיזים אלו לצורך הספקה בשר — מלבד כמויות וערית המועברות ליצאו נקניק.או לבשר בשחיטה "שחורה".

ואולם ככל שרב מספר העיזים השחורות כן גדל כבודן של בעליהן, השפעתו, מעמדו וסיכוייו לזכות ב...אשה יפה צעירה, בעיקר בקרב הבדווים...

משרדי הפנים והשרות לשמירת איכות הסביבה, שהעלו אתה את הנושא כזקוק לטיפול דחוף, מציינים כי ההידרדרות התחמורה שהחלה לאחר מלחמת ששת הימים ולאחר מלחמת יום הכיפורים, נובעת מכמה גורמים:

● שליטת עדרים מאיזור יהודה ושומרון לתחומ ,,הקו הירוק".

● עלייה בדווים מהנגב, שעשיו שותפויות עם בדווים מסיני, צפונה לאיזור הרי יהודה ואף לאיזור השרון.

● הבצורת בשנת 1972—73, ,,דחפה" כמויות גדולות של עדרים לאיזור הצפון. באותה שנה הסתבר לבדווים שאין בעזים שחורים דרומה, ולכן החל ,,להתיישב" קבע באזורים רבים.

● האפשרות למציאת תעסוקה (כגון עבודת שכירה

בחקלאות או מבתי־חרושת) לגברים במשפחה הנשים והילדים מוסיפים לרעות את העיזים, כש־ עובד כשכיר סמוד למקום המגורים.

● עירוד תושבי המרעה הגלון למרעה עיזים. בשנת היו בגולן 500 עיזים, היום יש למעלה מ־10,000 לציין שהכניסה אסרו גידול עזים פוחור[ות]

● הצבת גששים בדווים על־ידי צה"ל בא שונים ומתן אפשרויות לגששים לשכן את משפ ועדריהם. באזורים שבהם היה אסור כניסתם קודם

גורמים אלה הביאו לעלייה דראסטית ב העיזים השחורות — וזאת כאשר עלייה זו אינה ב עלייה מקבילה בשטחי מרעה. כתוצאה מכך עומק הרעיה על שטחי מרעה טבעיים והם נוצל כדי השמדות חורשים. אגב, רעיית עיזים שחורות אלה הינה בלתי־חוקית בדרך כלל ונעשית בש שנים ללא אישור כניסה אפשר. למעשה, אין על העיזים השחורות ומספיר לשלטות המרכזית ל טיסטיקה על גידול הענף אינם משקפים את המצ בעדרים רבים העיזים אינם נושאות תוויתות ,,סמו משרד החקלאות.

הגידול בענף, נשען על השטחים שבתחום, הירוק בעיקר, משום שמקורות המרעה בגדה מדולדדלים.

באיזור הגליל חלה עלייה גדולה ב ראשי העיזים בשל עלייה גדולה במספר הבשר וב ובשל העדר כח־אדם מספיק לפקח ולשמור לבל ה עדרים לשטחים אסורים.

בעיה נוספת היא חוסר האמצעים לקים וטרינרי על עדרי העיזים, דבר שעלול לגרום לה מחלות רבות. בפעל יש קיום לכל טיפול וטרינרי ב התעבצות ממקום למקום עלול לגרום נזק רב ל החי בישובים הקלאיים. כדי לזכות ברווחים קלים מ קלאים באזורים שונים שפחים למרעה לבני־המי . דבר זולה לחוק ולתקנות מיגנה מרקעיט יש יותר על כן. בישובים יהודיים, שבהם נערכת לא לגידול עיזים שחורות, נמסרו העיזים לבעלי ב הבדווים, אלה הכפילו ואף שלישו את כמות ה תוך חלוקת רווחים בין השותפים.

לדעת הגורמים המטפלים, יש לחסל את על־ידי הכנת תכנית רב־שנתיות לחיסול שטחי מ העיזים — על פי חוק כדוגמת ארצות אחרות — מתן פיצויים לבעליהן.

Fire on the Mountain. On December 2, 2010, a forest fire broke out on the Mount Carmel ridge. The fire spread quickly due to east winds and the vegetation being parched as a result of a rainless winter. The largest natural disaster in the State of Israel to date, the fire lasted four days and consumed more than 30,000 hectares of planted forest and natural woods—an estimated four million trees; it left the state in shock after 44 Prison Authority cadets were killed when their bus, on its way to evacuate a prison on the Carmel Range, caught fire. Furthermore, thousands of residents of the area were evacuated from their homes, and much property was lost to the flames.

The fate of animals was mixed. Those that were part of the Hai-Bar, a 6,000 hectare nature reserve used for breeding, as well as the livestock of nearby farms, were evacuated or rescued. The wildlife had no such luck, and it is impossible to know how many animals were killed. Those that escaped lost their habitat, and had to survive in a fierce competition for living space and food in the months that followed.

The fire revealed the poor state of fire services in Israel, and led to the establishment of a committee to reexamine forestry policies.

Burnt trees after a forest fire on Mount Carmel, 2010 (photo: Zvi Singer)

The Return of the Black Goat. The 2010 Mt. Carmel wildfire was the most dramatic and damaging in a series of fires that struck Israeli forests. Following the recurring fires, scientists and foresters reexamined forest management policies and radically changed their views toward goat grazing and its ecological benefits. Following long debates, the state shifted its attitude regarding the raising of black goats.

In the wake of the Carmel catastrophe, the government ordered a survey of ways to control forest fires, and one of the committee's main recommendations was to change forestry regulations and support regulated black goat grazing to reduce forest brush and control its growth.

The research on the virtues of grazing was not new. In fact, years back, in 1978, several ecologists protested the creation of a "Green Patrol" in 1976 that intensified the state's enforcement of grazing restrictions. In a letter to *the Jerusalem Post* daily, these ecologists argued that the implementation of the Black Goat Law had damaged ecological systems and stressed the merits of regulated grazing. In the past twenty years, extensive ecological research has demonstrated that regulated goat grazing not only prevents forest fires, but positively contributes to the biodiversity of forests and meadows.

Letter to the Editor,
In Defense of the Black Goat
Prof. M. Evenari, Prof. I. Noy-Meir and Prof. Z. Naveh
The Jerusalem Post, 1978

As ecologists whose work is related to natural vegetation and pasture, we have read the editorial on May 31, 1978 about "The Green Patrol," and the articles "Understanding the Bedouin" on May 31, 1978 and "A Painful Problem in the Negev" on June 2, 1978, with great interest. We applaud your positive attitude toward finding a solution to the difficult problem, and your criticism of the attempt to resolve it hastily through rigid, drastic measures that surely cause great human suffering [...].

Some of the facts which you take for granted, however, require further examination. In recent months, the public has received a constant stream of information about the tremendous damage and dangers caused by the Bedouin and their herds in all areas of our lives. In the field where our profession as ecologists enables us to examine the data independently [...], we have found that the reports are rife with half-truths, exaggerations, and unjustified generalizations.

Take, for example, one sentence from the editorial: "The destructive black goat." This animal indeed has had a poor reputation since the days of the scapegoat and he-goat shaped devil, and it has become one of the main targets in the actions of the Green Patrol against the Bedouin. Res. Gen. Avraham Yaffe has repeatedly vowed to exterminate the black goat from our country, believing this is the only way to protect our natural vegetation from goat induced extinction.

Goats differ from sheep and cattle as they feed on bushes and trees, but today the majority of ecologists (in Israel and elsewhere) think that the allegations against the goat in the past were largely exaggerated. The following are some points in defense of the black goat:

1. A goat that nibbles a shrub, does not kill it, but only trims it. The shrubs can grow back, bloom, and reproduce, even when there is a constant presence of goats on site (unless the goat population is too dense, in which case every shrub is eaten too often—a state of overgrazing).

2. Goat grazing prevents the shrubs and trees from taking over the entire area, driving out and eradicating the grassy plants—including beneficial pasture grasses and beautiful wildflowers—as well as the various species of animals and birds that require open spaces and herbaceous vegetation. So the black goat plays a role in maintaining biodiversity and balance in nature, a role which, under the local conditions, no other animal seems to be able to play successfully. (In some parts of Australia and the United States goats are actively introduced to prevent the devaluation of pasture for sheep and cattle).

3. The black goat has been part of the landscape and culture of the Land of Israel since biblical times. Our ecosystems, from desert to forest, are well adapted to goat grazing. Within certain boundaries, as far as we know, the "delicate natural balance" (a quote from your editorial), in which the black goats have lived for thousands of years (in our ecosystems)—the same balance can be equally violated by dramatically reducing the number of goats, just as much as by their overpopulation.

4. The black goat, for its part, is well adapted to live in hilly, dry areas with bushy vegetation. It produces milk and meat mainly by a diet of woody and thorny plants, which have no other economic use. The meat and milk produced by pasture-fed black goats cost the national economy less than imported fodder, and less foreign currency than any other animal-derived protein that we can produce or import.

5. In light of all the above, the black goat has a place in the country's uncultivated lands, and a crucial role in terms of both use and conservation of nature.

The Goat Law of 1950, whose full implementation will, in effect, eradicate the black goat, is based on outdated conceptions. This law ought to be reconsidered (the law was not implemented at all until November 1977, and since then, the Green Patrol has been increasingly busy enforcing it).

The danger is posed not by the black goat, but by uncontrolled exploitation of pasture land. The problem is not how to get rid of the black goat, but how to keep it in a controlled environment to prevent overgrazing in pasture land. There are solutions to this problem, but they require more patient, constructive, and thorough actions than merely launching the Green Patrol.

The capacity and productivity of our pasture lands, including those in the Negev, can be greatly increased by improved pasture management for the benefit of the state and the herd owners alike. The necessary professional knowledge exists in Israel, and has often been exported to solve similar problems in African and Asian countries. In solving our Bedouin problems, however, it seems that the application of professional knowledge in the fields of ecology and pasture is not deemed unnecessary. Botanical evidence indicates that there is severe overgrazing in parts of Judea and Samaria, northern Sinai, and the territories around Beersheba (to which the Green Patrol sends the Bedouin). There is no significant overgrazing in the Negev Mountains from which the Bedouins are driven away.

That's all about this aspect of the Bedouin problem. Obviously, there are other aspects of even greater national importance. Each must be carefully examined to distinguish facts from imagination.

Protocol of Knesset Session of 7 May 2018

*Plant Protection Bill (Damage by Goats, Cancellation), 2018
Second and third readings*

Knesset Speaker Yuli-Yoel Edelstein: We now move to the Plant Protection Bill (Damage by Goats, Cancellation), 2018, for a second and a third readings. The Chairman of the Economics Committee, MK Eitan Cabel, will present the bill. Please sir.

Eitan Cabel (Chairman of the Economics Committee): I am honored to bring to the Knesset for the second and third readings the Plant Protection Bill (Damage by Goats, Cancellation), 2018. The bill, which is a private bill by Knesset Member Jamal Zahalka—and I would like to congratulate him—proposes to repeal the Plant Protection Law (Damage by Goats), 1950. It is a law that was enacted in 1950, which states restrictions on the possession and grazing of goats, criminal offenses for violating the provisions of the law, as well as supervisory powers under which an inspector was authorized to seize goats if their number exceeded the permitted rate in respect of either grazing or keeping.

In practice, the grazing of goats helps reduce the risk of fire. Moreover, since the number of goats in Israel is smaller than desired today, not only is the law not actually implemented, but it

---

In 2018, the growing public awareness with regard to forest fires led to a one-time merging of interests, and made strange bedfellows in the Israeli parliament for a brief moment. Extreme right-wing politicians, who support forestry as a means of land control, and left wing Israeli-Palestinian members of parliament, found themselves working together, with different concerns, to formulate the legislation that repealed the Black Goat Act of 1950.

has clearly become unnecessary. It is therefore proposed to repeal the law. I would like to thank Attorney Naama Daniel for formulating this important law. You are lucky—you will be mentioned in one breath with the law passed by Zahalka; thanks are also due to the committee members. As you can see, there are no reservations, and this is truly an important law. Thank you very much.

Speaker Yuli-Yoel Edelstein: Members of the Knesset, we now move to a third reading. Who's in favor? Who's against? Please vote.

Vote #7

In favor – 37

Against – 0

Abstentions – 0

The Plant Protection Law (Damage by Goats, Cancellation), 2018—was passed.

Speaker Yuli-Yoel Edelstein: 37 votes in favor, 0 against, 0 abstentions.

Jamal Zahalka (Joint List): Finally, equality to goats. The black goat has been legitimized and can now be raised without restrictions, just like the white goat. It is a festive day for black goats and black goat keepers. I think this is one of the shortest laws ever passed in the Knesset. One single sentence—the Black Goat Law is repealed.

Plant Protection (Damage by Goats, Cancellation) Law—2018

Passed by the Knesset on the 22nd Iyar, 5778 (7th May, 2018). The Bill and an Explanatory Note were published in Hatza'ot Chok HaKnesset no. 759 of the 27th Shvat, 5778 (12th February, 2018), p. 96 [Hebrew].

Repeal of Plant Protection (Damage by Goats) Law	1. The Plant Protection (Damage by Goats) Law, 5710–1950, is hereby repealed.
Amendment of the Agricultural Control Authority Law, No. 3	2. In the Agricultural Control Authority Law, 5748–1988, in the Annex, Item 2 shall be deleted.
Amendment of the National Parks, Nature Reserves, National Sites and Memorial Sites Law, No. 16	3. The National Parks, Nature Reserves, National Sites and Memorial Sites Law, 5748–1988, in the Annex, Item 6 shall be deleted.
Amendment of the Regulation of the Kinneret Beaches Law, No. 2	4. In the Regulation of the Kinneret Beaches Law, 5768–2008, in the 2nd Annex, Item 10 shall be deleted.

Benjamin Netanyahu
Prime Minister

Uri Ariel
Minister of Agriculture and Rural Development

Reuven Rivlin
President of the State

Yuli-Yoel Edelstein
Speaker of the Knesset

The Kensset session, 7 May 2018

High Waters
Chapter 3

The Water Buffalo.

The water buffalo (Arabic *Jamus*) is a large mammal of the Bovidae family. Domesticated, humans harness it to a plow, drink its milk, and eat its meat.

Fog blurs the trail of the buffalo's journey from East Asia to the territory of Israel-Palestine. Some claim it appeared in the Bible as "kine of Bashan," or in the Talmud as "kvi"/"koy" (cow?) or "wild ox," but evidence for this identification is weak and there is no conclusive proof of their existence in Palestine before the Middle Ages. It is generally assumed that water buffaloes arrived in the country with the Muslim conquests in the 8th century CE, and that they acclimated successfully and provided the locals with their sweet, fatty milk.

Due to poor thermal tolerance, the buffalo tends to live near shallow water sources, especially marshlands, hence it is not used in industrialized agriculture. This proclivity also determined its local habitats: the Huleh marshlands, the Yarkon, the Na'aman Valley, and Kebarah. Ottoman taxation lists indicate a widespread distribution of water buffaloes in the 16th century, and almost all tourists and pilgrims who visited the Holy Land mentioned them in their memoirs.

The water buffalo disappeared from the local landscape with the transition to industrialized agriculture, concurrent with the large water projects introduced by Zionism: the Yarkon water was diverted to the desert (the Yarkon-Negev Project, 1950), Lake Huleh and its marshes were drained (1951–1958), and so was the Kebarah marshland. The landscape changed, the habitat was destroyed, great big machines were brought into the fields, and the large beast disappeared from the land.

Water buffaloes wallowing in the Huleh swamp, first half of the 20th century »

In the early 20th century, there were more than 5,000 water buffaloes around Lake Huleh and its marshland. Water buffaloes also lived on the banks of the Yarkon and Na'aman rivers and the Kebarah marshland.

The water buffalo's large, watery eyes reflect the lake and the marsh, the water lilies and the reeds. He is entirely under water, only his head sticking out—his damp nose gleams in the sun's rays, and his horns are large and crescent shaped.

The Land and the Book
William McClure Thomson, 1854

This pool is crowded with buffaloes; and how oddly they look, with nothing but the nose above water! Yes; and observe that their mouths are all turned up stream toward the fountain, and on a level with the surface, as if, like Job's behemoth, they trust that they can draw up Jordan into their mouths.

William McClure Thomson (1806–1894), an American Protestant missionary who spent 25 years working in Ottoman Syria, published a best-selling account of his travels.

A Journey to the Holy Land: Life of St. Willibald
724

They breed remarkable cattle there, long in the back, short in the leg, and with huge horns. They are all the same colour, purple. In that place there are deep swamps, so when summer comes, and the sun is very hot and scorches the land, these cattle move over to the swamps, and submerge their whole body, with only their head sticking out.

St. Willibald (700–787) was a bishop of Eichstättin, Bavaria, and the first known Englishman to visit the Holy Land.

268 ‹ The Water Buffalo ›

BABEER CANE.

THE BUFFALO.

Popular Arab Song

The sun has risen,   طلعت يا محلا نورها
oh so very beautiful,   شمس الشمّوسة

Come on. Lets go out   يلّا بنا نملا ونحلب
to milk the she-buffalo   لبن الجاموسة

The water buffalo and papyrus at the Huleh swamp (illustrations from Thomson's *The Land and the Book*, 1854)

270 ‹ The Water Buffalo ›

Water buffaloes harnessed to a plow, 1940 (photo: Zoltan Kluger)

271

The Ghawarne people harvesting papyrus reeds
for the weaving of mats, 1946 (photo: Zoltan Kluger)

The Swamp.

The Gates of Jerusalem
R. Moshe Reicher, 1867

> A long river, its course three hours and one hour in breadth. Many a forest along its banks, and it is trampled by wild animals too. In summer, the Jordan river bed often dries up and becomes arid, and in the month of Nisan it is filled with water from the Lebanon snow, its waters very turbid.

Schare Jerusalem (The Gates of Jerusalem) by **R. Moshe Reicher** is a collection of homiletic interpretations (*midrashim*) describing the Land of Israel in the mid-19th century from a Jewish point of view.

The Huleh lake and swamps, aerial photos, 1945 (collage: Bar Mussan Levi) »

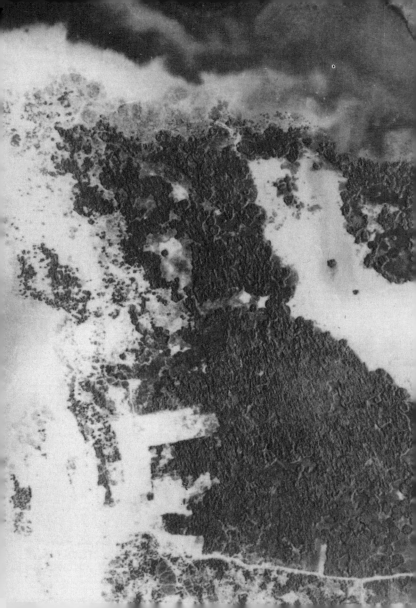

Aerial view of the Huleh Valley, 1938 (photo: Zoltan Kluger)

Paddling in the Huleh
Moshe Gershoni, 1954

Summer tour in the heart of the marshland—one of many. Five of us headed for the swamp. We opened a path through the tangled reed thicket. Our destination—the little pools we saw from the Nabi Yusha summit. It is not easy to reach a destination at the middle of the swamp. One must be blessed with an excellent sense of orientation, sometimes a compass and advanced planning. Because once you penetrate the heart of the swamp, you are surrounded by a thick, dark grove, with no horizon; reed inflorescences rise over your head and all around you, and you can see nothing but the extent of your touch. The cool waters of the swamp flow south, there is no solid ground under your feet, and you sink, time and again, into the humid carpet of decayed vegetation, which will eventually become peat. It took several hours to advance a mere few hundred meters in the terrible bush of vegetation. Every step was achieved by force, with the crushed reeds trampled into a path through which we move forward.

Finally, when [...] our feet stood on the edge of one of the coveted pools, we all froze before it, our eyes wide open, our mouth agape, breathing deeply, in wonder at the absorbing beauty [...]. We arrived at the chain of pools [...], and here is a description of one of them: 30x50 meters in size, it is bedecked with a belt of cane and reeds at five meters high. Pool water is shallow, calm, clear and pure. Here and there, islands composed of giant leaves have floated to the surface of the water, concealing pristine white lilies beneath them—the renowned Nymphaea.

Moshe Gershoni (1918-2007), a teacher and pedagogue, founder of the school in Kibbutz Hulata.

Floating forest. Papyrus growing in the Huleh swamps, 1951

The Jordan River meandering through the Huleh swamp, ca. 1960 (photo: Peter Merom)

282 ‹ The Swamp ›

John MacGregor (1825–1892) was an adventure traveler and a pioneer of the sport of canoeing, who introduced the kayak into Europe. His adventures took him across the world, including the Middle East. His descriptions of his travels in his 'canoes,' each named Rob Roy after the family's historic namesake, became immensely popular. The expedition from the Nile to the Jordan River and the Sea of Galilee, described in *The Rob Roy on the Jordan,* was his best-known work.

THE
ROB ROY ON THE JORDAN,

NILE, RED SEA, & GENNESARETH, &c.

A CANOE CRUISE IN PALESTINE AND EGYPT, AND THE WATERS OF DAMASCUS.

BY J. MACGREGOR, M.A.

THIRD EDITION.

WITH MAPS AND ILLUSTRATIONS.

LONDON:
JOHN MURRAY, ALBEMARLE STREET.
1870.

The right of Translation is reserved.

into a sort of imperishable leather were soon dissolved into a mass of black meaningless jelly.[6]

Next day was devoted to a strict examination of the northern side of Merom, and very soon on turning into one of the deep bays in the papyrus, I noticed a sensible current in the water. In a moment every sense was on the *qui vive*, and with quick-beating heart and earnest paddle-strokes I entered what proved to be *the mouth of Jordan*.

At this place the papyrus is of the richest green, and upright as two walls on either hand, and so close is its forest of stems and dark recurving hair-like tops above that no bird can fly into it, and the very few ducks that I found had wandered in by swimming through the chinks below, were powerless to get wing for rising; so while their flappings agitated the jungle, and their cackling shrieks told loudly how much they wished to escape from the intruder, the birds themselves were entirely invisible, though only a few yards from me all the time. But they were safe enough from any stranger, for in no part could I ever get the point of the Rob Roy to enter three feet into the dense hedge of this wonderful floating forest.

The Jordan's mouth here is a hundred feet wide, and it is entirely concealed from both shores by a bend it makes to the east. The river thus enters the lake at the *end* of a promontory of papyrus, and one can understand that

---

[6] The captured head, which has curly feathers, was shown (with other curiosities of this voyage) at the Exhibition held in the Egyptian Hall by the Exploration Fund, as remarkable on account of its size, the manner of its capture, and the place where it was taken The Arabs call the pelican "Mjah," and sometimes "Jemel el Bahr," that is, "sea camel," which well describes its manner of carrying the head with the neck in a double arch. Besides those that fly by the sea, and the Nile, and the Lake Merom, the pelican is found upon other lonely ponds. Finn states that one was killed in Solomon's Pools, near Jerusalem.

The New-found Mouth of Jordan.

286 ‹ The Swamp ›

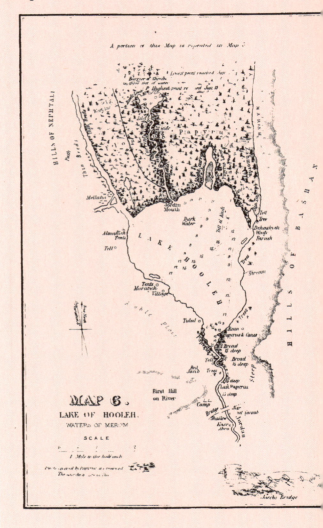

this projection is caused by the plants growing better where the water runs than in the still parts, so that the walls or banks of green are prolonged by the current itself. Once round the corner, and entering the actual river, it is a wonderful sight indeed as the graceful channel winds in ample sweeps or long straight reaches in perfect repose and loneliness with a soft silent beauty all its own

Recovering from the first excitement of this important discovery, I set about recording all its features in a methodical way. First, of course, by counting paddle-strokes, as we slowly mounted the stream, then by noting the bends right and left in my book, and the few tributaries that entered on this side and that. On the west, one joined which might have been easily mistaken for the true channel, but happily recollecting that in my sketch made from the mountain this arm from the west ends in nothing, I went steadily up the other Presently a strange noise came out of the foliage, and, approaching cautiously, I found two great falcons or water-eagles feeding on something in their nest on an islet. The Rob Roy at once "beat to quarters," but when her crew attempted to "board," out rushed the male bird, and screamed and whirled about me so defiant that "discretion was the better part of valour," and the nest was left alone.

A few tiny sparrow-like birds hovered here and there on the papyrus tops, and two or three divers swam a yard or so in the open, and then rose and went out of sight; but the solitary silence of the place was almost painful, and it begot a feeling of awe when nothing but green jungle was present on every side, and yet I was glad no other man was there—not from churlish jealousy, but for his own sake too, who might wish to enjoy this scene—let him come also, but free from me, and at some other time. The paddle in new places is best enjoyed alone, just as the fishing-rod or the exciting tale.

The channel narrowed at 800 double strokes (about 4000 yards), and the current sharpened, too, and I confess that here I was almost about to return, from some vague unaccountable fear, or weariness, or presentiment that I was to be lost in the maze of green; it seemed then so far to have gone away from life and light outside, and in so short a time. Very often since have I rejoiced that more bravery came, and the resolve at least to rest and think, before returning. So the Rob Roy clung to the shady side of the channel, and then a long and glorious peal of thunder rolled athwart the sky.

I have listened to that deep-toned voice when standing on a volcano's crater—when gazing at night on the falls of Niagara—and when sailing alone in the hurtlings of a midnight storm on the breakers at Beachy Head. These were, indeed, splendid times and places for hearing in the depths of one's mind the loud speaking that comes out of the unseen. But none of them was so perfectly new and strange as this one single roar from heaven, shaking the vast quiet of Hooleh.

An immediate effect of it was to awaken energy and to nerve me to go on, so as at least to accomplish the round sum of 1000 double paddle-strokes. But before doing so, an old newspaper I had cast on the river, and which now floated along, suggested the idea of measuring the speed of the current. For this I cut a long papyrus stem into pieces of a few inches, and carefully scattered them across the channel and marked the time by my watch, so as to see how long would elapse before they were overtaken afterwards in our descent of the stream.

CHAP. XVII.]   *Inner Lake.*   293

This plan, however, though carefully worked, was futile, for I never saw one of my floats again.[7]

At 960 strokes, suddenly rounding a corner, I entered a beautiful little lake, just one you would picture in fancy. The general contour of it was round, but the edges were curved into deep bays, with dark alleys and bright projecting corners, while islets dotted the middle. Every single part of the boundary about me was green papyrus —not ragged and straggling, but upright and sharply defined. The breadth of this lake east and west was estimated at half a mile. Seen from the mountain, it appears certainly wider than that, but I have followed the MS. notes, entered at the time in my log.

Extreme caution was instantly prescribed by this novel scene, for without coolness and clear noting of the course, it might be difficult or impossible to find again the narrow entrance which must be passed through for return. Therefore, I bent down some of the tall green stems and tied them together, and placed upon them for a warning flag large slips of "the Supplement." Then carefully noting the compass bearings, I advanced to the next group of islands, and did the same again, always placing the beacons upon the right hand, so as to show the way out in returning. The lake was *perfectly* still—not "calm as a millpond," which expression often includes a shivering ruffle on the water, but with a smoothness like glass itself, and the water below was clear and without the slightest current. The lake was shallowed to five feet, but all the bottom was a soft carpet

[7] After much consideration, and as it was better to overrate the current than to overstate my advance into the papyrus, it appeared right to estimate the distance traversed by each double stroke of the paddle here at four yards instead of five and a half, and this part of the map, therefore, is constructed upon that reduced scale.

of delicate water-moss, patterned in pretty green network. Large yellow lilies floated on the surface in gay-coloured bouquets. I had seen many of these lilies along the north shore of the lake, but their stems were so thick and multitudinous below that, whenever I tried to drag up the very roots of them—if, indeed, they have any roots in the earth at all—the weight became quite unmanageable. However, I cut and brought home some portions of the complicated mass.

In the very centre of the lake, the canoe "heve to" for compass bearings. The sun was now very hot, but the air was cleared by the thunder. The view, so much contracted before by the high papyrus walls, now opened on all sides, for there was space about me.

To the north was the rounded head of splendid glittering Hermon, and to its left the far-off snow on the sharp indented Sunnin, chief of the Lebanon range. High on a lonely crag to the west was Neby Yusha, "Joshua's Tomb,"[8] and the eastern shore was girt by the "hill of Bashan."[9]

[8] Finn well reminds us that the welies may often be intended to honour Moslem "saints," who had Scripture names.

[9] In our sketch at p. 289, the two snow mountains are depicted. This sight of Senir and Lebanon, and the hills of Bashan, all at one time, and from a boat, reminds one of the beautiful verses in Ezekiel (ch. xxvii.), where the rich grandeur of Tyre is painted in language so magnificent, and the mountains now before us have a place :—

"Thus saith the Lord God; O Tyrus, thou hast said, I am of perfect beauty. "Thy borders are in the midst of the seas, thy builders have perfected thy beauty. "They have made all thy ship boards of fir trees of Senir : they have taken cedars from Lebanon to make masts for thee. "Of the oaks of Bashan have they made thine oars ; the company of the Ashurites have made thy benches of ivory, brought out of the isles of Chittim.

"Fine linen with broidered work from Egypt was that which thou spreadest forth to be thy sail ; blue and purple from the isles of Elishah was that which covered thee. "The inhabitants of Zidon and Arvad were

In the middle of all, and evidently as yet unconscious of my nearness, was one of the most graceful of living objects—a pure-white swan, floating upon the lovely lake, that mirrored his image again below. It never entered into my head to shoot him, pretty creature—that would have been sheer sacrilege: his tameness was quite shocking. But, just to waken up the echoes around us, and to give vent to the emotions of my mind, so long pent up in absolute silence, I fired a volley, and gave three cheers.

It was a very difficult thing to make quite sure that this little lake was a termination of the journey upwards; that it was not merely an enlargement of a stream which I had now resolved to follow up, *coûte que coûte*, to the end. But a careful circuit of its labyrinthine borders satisfied me that this is *the earliest flow of Jordan as one river* after it dives into the barrier whither I had traced it some days before. The north end of this lake was at 1130 double paddle-strokes from the mouth of the channel: that is, 6000 yards, or less than three miles and a half; and, allowing for current, it may be well averred that the Jordan aggregates its waters in this inner lake at the head of a channel which winds along nearly three miles before it enters the larger lake of Hooleh.

The interesting question as to the breadth of the impassable barrier could be settled only by a comparison between the observations made in my journey down the river in Map V. and those made now in this central lake, the northern end of which is marked

thy mariners: thy wise men, O Tyrus, that were in thee, were thy pilots. "The ancients of Gebal and the wise men thereof were in thee thy calkers: all the ships of the sea with their mariners were in thee to occupy thy merchandise.'

P in Map VI. By a point in each map given in the MS. survey of Captain Wilson, already noticed, we were able to place them so that it may be seen that the interval between N and P—that is, the breadth of the barrier—is about half a mile.[10]

The journey back along the new channel was pleasant and easy, and lasted less than an hour. My various beacons all were spied, and, to guide the next canoeist, they were left there; but with the keenest look-out, I could not discover any one of the current-floats which had been so carefully strewn for the purpose, and only the floating newspaper could be discerned on the gliding stream. This, however, did not help me to estimate the current, because the time and place of its starting had not been noted. As a rough guess, I should say that Jordan's current here is, at the most, about a mile in an hour.

At the mouth again, all safe, the Rob Roy was moored for luncheon in the shade, and never was a roast fowl eaten with a heartier relish than after such a morning's work.

Next she entered a bay farther eastwards, but this quickly narrowed and ran up into a *cul de sac* at 2000 yards, until I could pass only through a narrow gap into deep gloomy waterways, without any stream, and where the tall papyrus stems were tangled over my head. Still I followed this up to its positive termination, and with all the precautions (as to beacons and guide-marks) so useful before; and again the canoe came back into the light, where, in the green circuit of the bay once more, I

[10] For observations as to latitude, I was dependent entirely on one bearing of Neby Yusha, seen from point P, but the distance estimate from paddle-strokes may well be considered to transfer the measurement to the mouth of the river in the lake, and so to connect it with the survey of the lake itself.

found, in one group of graceful elegance, sixteen wild swans swimming together. Beautiful as they were, it was well to have seen that one swan first before meeting so many. Again a salute from the pistol stunned the air, and all the white beauties rose up in terror or high dudgeon; their wavy circlings above me cleft the sky with bright gleaming tracks for a moment, and they passed away like a vision.

As the Rob Roy neared the open lake, it was felt that the wind had risen very suddenly, and this soon explained a most curious hissing, grinding, bustling sound, that was heard like waves upon a shingly beach. For, in delighted surprise, I found that the margin of the lake about me was waving up and down, and the papyrus stems were rubbing against each other as they nodded out and in. It was plain in a moment that the whole jungle of papyrus was *floating upon the water*, and so the waves now raised by the breeze were rocking the heavy green curtain to and fro.

My soundings had shown the depth in Jordan's channel to be almost uniform, at from twelve to ten feet, all the way up; and at first it seemed strange that there should be any special current in one part, when the water had apparently a wide way to run through underneath the floating field. But the reason of this is soon apparent when we know how the papyrus grows; and as the vast area of it now before us is believed to be the largest mass of papyrus in the world, it may be a proper time to look at this strange plant here.

The papyrus plant is called "Babir" by the Arabs of Hooleh, which is as near the Latin word as can be, considering that the Arabs use *b* for *p*. In Arabic its name is Berdi, and in Hebrew Gôme, a word used four times in the Bible. In the Septuagint the word παπυρος is used. The name *Papyrus* still survives in the English name of the material upon which these words are printed. For reeds in general the Hebrew term is Kaneh.

The papyrus stem is three-cornered; in this feature it is one of a limited number of plants. The thicker and taller stems are not at the edge, but about five or six feet inwards; therefore I was unable to get at them without incurring great danger. Also, as I meant to bring out the largest possible specimen, the endeavour was often put off until finally the opportunity had passed. The sketch given here shows the manner of growth of this plant. There is first a lateral trunk, A, lying on the water, and half-submerged.[11] This is often as thick as a man's body, and from its lower side hang innumerable string-like roots from three to five feet long and of a deep purple colour. It is these pendent roots that retard so much of the surface-current where the papyrus grows, as noticed above for explanation. On the upper surface of the trunks the stems grow alter-

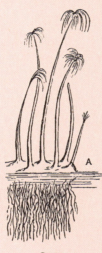

Papyrus.

[11] The woodcut in Smith's 'Dictionary of the Bible' represents the *stalks* as under water, but the natural free growth of the plant seems to me from a floating trunk, and this would only be submerged exceptionally. The small flowerets on the hairy threads of the *thyrsus* top in Smith's sketch are not seen in winter. The sketch of papyrus given by Dr. Thomson does not show its multitude of tall stems. The papyrus represented by a steel engraving in 'Bruce's Travels' is very accurate. See also *ante*, p. 78, note.

Chap. XVII.] *Its Use.* 299

nately in oblique rows; their thickness at the junction is often four inches, and their height fifteen feet, gracefully tapering until at the top is a little round knob, with long, thin, brown, wire-like hairs eighteen inches long, which rise and then, recurving, hang about it in a thyrsus-shaped head. The stem, when dead, becomes dark brown in colour, and when dry, it is extremely light; indeed, for its strength and texture, it is the lightest substance I know of.

The papyrus was used for writing upon by the Egyptians, and was prepared for this purpose by cutting it into thin slips. These were laid side by side, and upon them others in a cross direction, and both were joined by cement and then pressed into a continuous sheet. It is obvious that by this means the length, and to a certain extent the breadth, of a papyrus roll might be made according to pleasure.

The Ethiopians made boats of papyrus. Ludolf says that these boats are used in the Tzamic Lake, and Moses was hid in a vessel made of this.[12] I have seen a woman put her baby on a bundle of reeds and swim across the Nile while she pushed it along. The plant is mentioned in a beautiful passage of Isaiah (chap. xxxv. 7), and in Job it is asked, "Can the papyrus grow up without mire?" (chap. viii. 11). Herodotus says that the papyrus was eaten after being stewed. This *Papyrus antiquorum* is not now found in Egypt, nor anywhere in Asia except in Syria. But it grows 7° from the Equator in Nubia, on the White Nile. This singular plant is traced along the Jordan only a short distance (post

[12] Dr. Thomson ('Land and the Book,' p. 337) says the process described in Exodus ii. 3, may mean that the ark was "bitumed" by the mixture, so as to resemble a coffin, and thereby to enable the mother to take her child out of the house.

p. 306), and then it reappears at Ain et Tin, on the Sea of Galilee, and is also said to be found on the River Aujeh, near Jaffa; but I did not observe it in the part I examined of that river. Another kind (*Papyrus syriacus*) is cultivated in our botanical gardens, and is found wild on the plain of Sharon.[13]

It is not difficult to understand how the papyrus grove is so very thick just at its boundary edge, whereas reeds, or rushes, or other aquatic plants, usually get sparse and stunted or broken down all round the borders of a marsh, or where it merges into open water.

This peculiarity, which gives to the papyrus plain of Hooleh its most remarkable feature of upright wall-like sides—and that, too, on deep water—is caused, I think, by the manner of the plant's growth. Such of the lateral stems as shoot out into open water become bent or broken by waves, and so they bind in the rest, and the outer stems have too much wind and rough weather to flourish as well as the others do inside, which are well protected. This may be noticed even more distinctly when the papyrus grows in running water, as in that part of the marsh through which the Jordan flows. But while we remark that the plant seems to thrive best where the water is not stagnant, and so the largest stems are near the channel of the river, it may be asked why they do not spread across the actual channel. The sketch annexed will explain this at once. It is a bird's-eye view of several of the lateral trunks, which are represented as being turned by the force of the current all in one direction—that of the arrow, S—and so, gradually bending round to the positions R, T, U, they at last fold

---

[13] Dr. Tristram, in the 'Leisure Hour,' 1866, p. 553. Thomson probably alludes to the latter kind when he mentions papyrus in the river Fulej, near the Aujeh ('Land and the Book,' p. 512).

CHAP. XVII.]   *Bent by Current.*   301

upon, encircle, and strangle their neighbours, and seriously hinder their growth. The width of the clear channel is therefore kept at a uniform relation to the speed of the current; for if that is slow, it allows the trunks to spread and to cover the surface, and with their roots to narrow the channel until the speed of the stream is thereby increased, and the trunks are by it curved, stunted, and thus worn off, and so a just balance is regained.

The amount of water exhaled by the evaporation from millions of these stems, presenting so large an area of surface above, must be prodigious, although, on the other hand, the shade of their thick darkness keeps the direct rays of the sun from striking into the water itself. So much for the papyrus.

Papyrus.

The Rob Roy then entered every little bight along the indented edge, to make perfectly sure that no other open channel was to be discovered, until at length she came to the eastern coast of the lake. Here I peeped round the cape, but no Arab was in sight at the moment, for they don't like wind; but I was too tired with work and the excitement of discovery to venture upon a longer journey here, so our bows turned back across the open water to the hovels of Mataryeh, whither our camp had been ordered to move.

Fauna & Flora of Huleh.

Lake Huleh and its marshes were noted for their unique biodiversity. This was the southern distribution boundary of the Euro-Siberian fauna and flora, also spanning animals from warmer southern regions. Many animals lived in the lake and in the swamp thicket: seven different species of tilapia, different species of barbel and catfish, as well as many mammals, such as otter, jackal, buffalo, mongoose, jungle cat, wild boar, and various rodents; and reptiles—various species of turtles; and amphibians, including the endemic species of a Huleh painted frog. Passing birds stopped here during migration season on their way from Europe to Africa and back. Among the fowl were the cormorant, the coot, the common moorhen, various species of herons, shorebirds, grebes, ducks, storks, and more. There were songbirds and raptors in the reed thicket, including the white-tailed eagle, found locally only in Huleh.

It was a vast and diversified habitat that included not only the animals living in the marsh itself, but also those coming to drink water and enjoy the tremendous biological abundance; even the Syrian bear came down from Mount Hermon to drink from the cool lake and catch fish in the shallow water.

Storks at Lake Huleh, 1961 (photo: Peter Merom)

Cyperus papyrus

301

Hydrocotyle ranunculoides

302 ‹ **Fauna & Flora of Huleh** ›

Scirpus lacustris

Nuphar lutea

304 ‹ Fauna & Flora of Huleh ›

Nymphaea alba

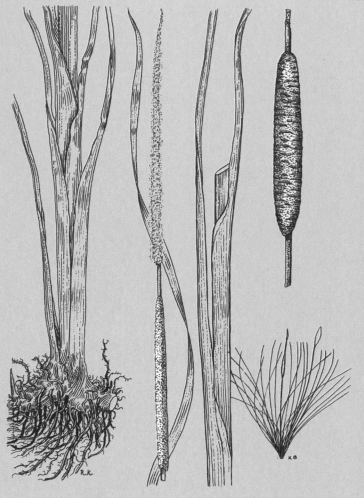

Typha domingensis

Settlers.

From the mid-19th century onward, Jewish settlers began to colonize the Huleh Valley near the Sea of Galilee.

Jewish visitors (Justus and Gretel Saalheimer, Maly Simon) at Lake Huleh, with an unidentified Arab oarsman, 1935

At the Huleh on the day concession was approved to drain the lake and swamps by the Jewish National Fund (JNF/KKL), 1934 (photo: Zvi Oron)

308 ‹ Settlers ›

Hunting in Lake Huleh, 1935

The Draining Project.

Over the years, the opinion has taken root that the peat at the bottom of the marsh holds great potential for intensive agricultural cultivation, and dreams of draining the swamp have begun, making the lake a real estate speculation. A concession to drain the marsh had already been awarded in Ottoman times, and passed from hand to hand. In the wake of World War I, the area was handed over to the British mandatory authorities until, in 1934, the concession was acquired by the Palestine Land Development Company (PLDC). Experts were brought in, detailed plans were drafted, maps drawn, and small-scale draining operations were initiated on several occasions—but the outbreak of World War II postponed the work.

After the establishment of the State of Israel, and in view of the great waves of immigration, the need for new farmland increased, and in 1951 the draining operations were launched.

Huleh Basin Report
Rendel, Palmer and Trotton, 1936

The preliminary inspection had shown that the survey of the marsh area would be the most difficult part of the work. The method proposed for the survey of the bed of the lake and marshes was to set out lines across them at regular intervals and take soundings along these lines: in the lake where a boat could be used this work would present no difficulty, but in the marsh area as the papyrus was impassable for boats it would be necessary to cut narrow lanes through it along the survey lines. It was questionable, whether it would be possible to get these lanes cut, whether the cost would not be too great; in which case, some different method of survey would be necessary.

The services of the Arabs of Mallaha village, who were accustomed to cutting papyrus for making mats, were utilised, and several trials were made at cutting lanes through the marsh. [...] Although, lanes could be cut through the papyrus, boats could not traverse these, as under water there still existed a tangled mass of papyrus roots. A man could get along, however, by stepping on the papyrus roots at the risk of occasionally getting immersed. Eventually, lanes 1 km apart, extending in an easterly direction across the papyrus, were cut throughout the papyrus area. Jewish chainmen then measured the lines and took soundings at close intervals; soundings were taken on the soft mud and also through the mud onto the firm bed at a lower depth. Once the hot weather started the growth of the papyrus was so fast that in a month after cutting the lanes were almost completely obliterated, so it was fortunate that this work was started on March.

The Huleh Basin Report, submitted in July 1936, concluded the examination of the possibilities for draining the Huleh swamp and lake, and transforming them into agricultural land.

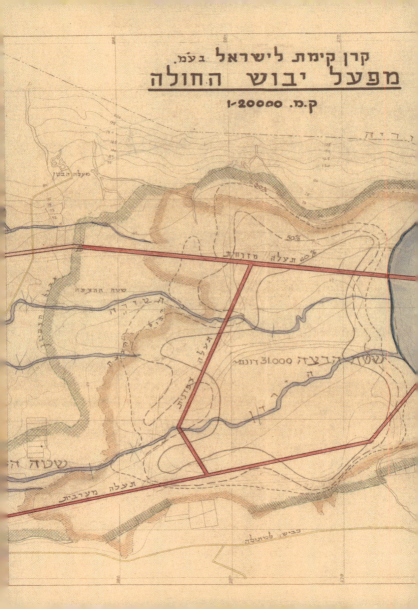

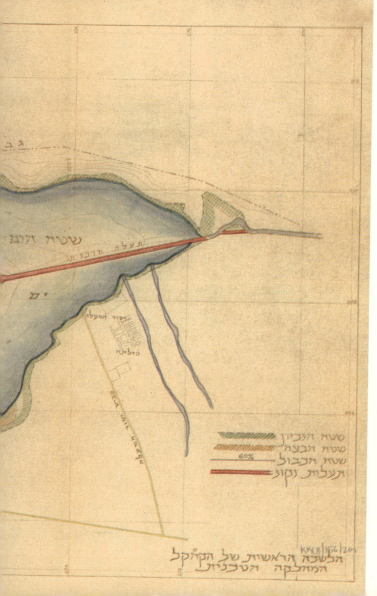

Huleh Draining Project: blueprint, 1941–42

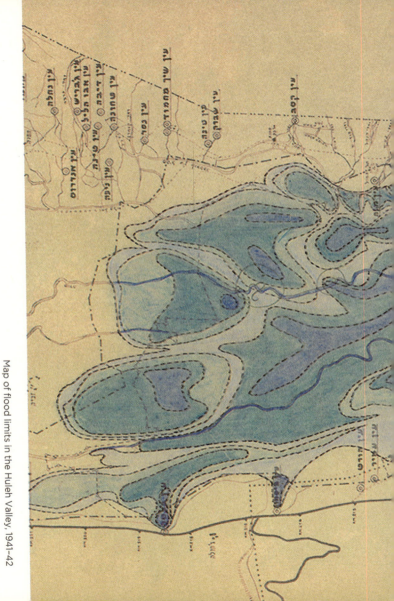

Map of flood limits in the Huleh Valley, 1941-42

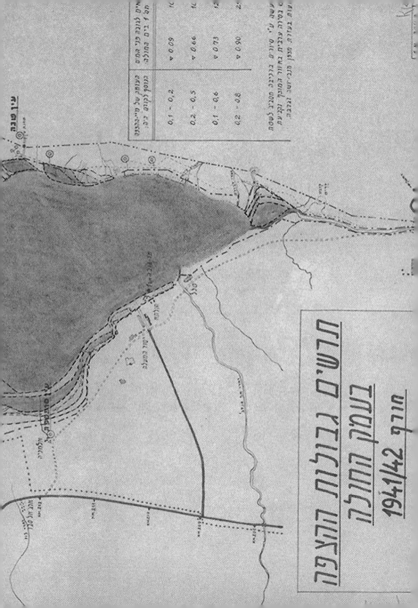

‹The Draining Project›

Field utilization chart and detailed livestock inventory in each village: left: details on the livestock of each village (cows, water buffalo, sheep, horses and mules, camels, donkeys and poultry); right: List of the Huleh Valley villages (Arab and Jewish) and the types of land they own (field crop, orchard, pasture, marshland)

טבלאות בעלות הקרקע באיזור החולה לפי הכפרים

	ערבי חוץ-לארץ		עתי הארץ		יהודים				שטח כללי	שמות הכפרים	
	פלחים	אפנדים	פלחים אמטים	פלחים	מרעי	חברות	פיק"א	קק"ל			
	1220	-	-	1697	-	-	1550	-	4467	(מפ) אבל אל-קמח	1.
	-	-	525	1050	-	-	-	-	2405	(פט) בוריה	2.
	-	-	2035	67	-	-	-	-	2102	(מפ) ביסמון	3.
	-	5300	-	-	-	-	-	-	5300	(מט) בלידה	4.
	136	2287	-	-	-	-	-	84	2507	(מפ) בנים	5.
	459	1190	-	-	-	-	-	3863	5512	(מט) ברג׳יאת	6.
	-	-	1350	1360	-	-	-	-	3860	(מט) ג׳חולה	7.
	-	540	-	-	-	-	-	-	540	(מט) ג׳לבינא	8.
	475	2978	-	-	-	-	-	-	3453	(מט) גרבה	9.
	405	-	-	2220	-	-	-	2925	5550	(מפ) דורה	10.
	-	762	-	-	-	-	-	-	762	(מפ) דיר מפט	11.
	-	-	-	-	-	-	-	4106	4106	(מפ) דובנה	12.
	1438	1445	-	-	-	-	-	-	2883	(מש) דרבסיה	13.
	-	544	-	-	-	-	-	1288	1288	(מט) דרדרא	14.
	1442	-	-	7682	-	-	-	2400	544	(מט) דריג׳ת	15.
	3124	-	-	831	-	-	-	-	11524	(מש) חונין	16.
	670	1992	-	-	-	-	-	-	3955	(מש) חורה	17.
	6900	-	-	2010	-	-	-	1680	2662	(מש) דוק אל פוקני	18.
	550	1000	-	14222	-	41162	-	-	10590	(מש) דוק את תחתני	19.
	-	655	-	-	-	-	-	-	56934	(מפ) זכירן החולה	20.
	-	-	-	155	-	-	-	4060	655	(מפ) הרה	21.
	500	-	-	10315	-	-	-	-	4215	(מפ) חים אל וליד	22.
	-	-	-	-	-	-	-	2317	10815	(מט) חלצה	23.
	-	-	450	2558	-	-	1400	300	2317	(מפ) חן אל-דויר	24.
	875	-	344	1314	251	-	-	2903	4708	(מפ) מסינה(תליל)	25.
									5687	(מט) תצר	26.
	-	-	-	-	-	-	4000	-	4000	(מפ) חרבת אם סמן (עין זגה)	27.
	-	-	-	-	-	10460	-	-	10460	(מפ) יסוד המעלה	28.
	-	-	-	-	-	5946	-	-	5946	(מפ) כפר גלעדי	29.
	-	-	0	260	-	-	-	1090	490	(מפ) כפר קילה	30.
	-	-	-	-	-	-	-	-	1550	(מט)+(מפ) לדדה	31.
	-	-	-	-	-	-	-	-	534	(מש) מבר אש סבען	32.
	-	-	-	-	-	-	-	480	730	(מש) מרתיל	33.
	-	-	-	-	-	5180	-	-	5180	(מפ) מטולה	34.
	-	-	-	-	-	-	-	-	12000	(מט) מיס	35.
	-	-	-	1827	-	-	900	-	2932	(מש) מלחה	36.
	-	-	-	10	-	-	-	136	1544	(מש) מנצורה	37.
	-	-	-	-	-	-	-	1560	3180	(מש) מנרה	38.
	-	-	-	1622	-	-	-	-	3703	(מש) מפתארה	39.
	-	-	-	3500	-	-	-	-	3500	(מש) נבי יושע	40.
	-	-	-	2397	-	-	-	2460	7157	(מפ) נעמה	41.
	-	-	-	-	-	-	-	-	2520	(מש) סברייה	42.
	-	-	-	1774	-	-	-	787	4795	(מפ)+(מש) עמטיה	43.
	-	-	-	-	-	-	-	-	2175	(מש) עדיסה	44.
	-	-	-	-	-	-	-	-	4000	(מט) עדנית	45.
	-	-	-	-	-	-	-	600	1800	(מש) עין פית	46.
	-	-	0	769	-	-	-	-	903	(מש) עין את תינה	47.
	-	-	-	-	-	-	-	-	1169	עלמניה	48.
	-	-	-	4462	-	-	-	797	5266	(מפ) צלחיה	49.
	-	-	-	465	-	-	-	7155	12620	(מש) קדש	50.
	-	-	-	3915	-	-	-	200	5315	(מש) קיטסיה	51.
	-	-	-	20	-	-	-	-	1570	(מש) שוקא את התתא	52.
			14	66502	251	41162	25436	45241	264380	ס"ה	

Table of land ownership in the Huleh area according to villages, distinguishing between Jewish-owned land (JNF, PICA, corporate, and private ownership) and "local Arabs" and "foreign Arabs"

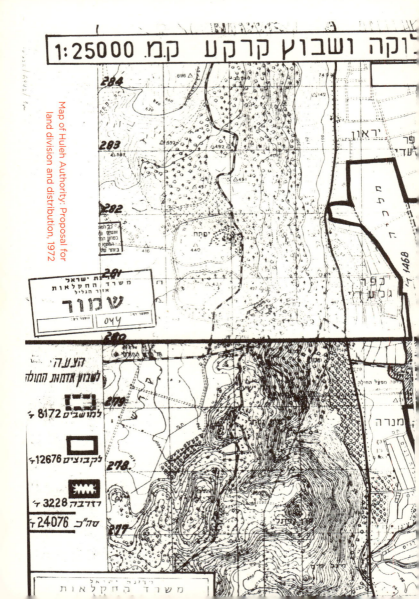

Map of Huleh Authority: Proposal for land division and distribution, 1972

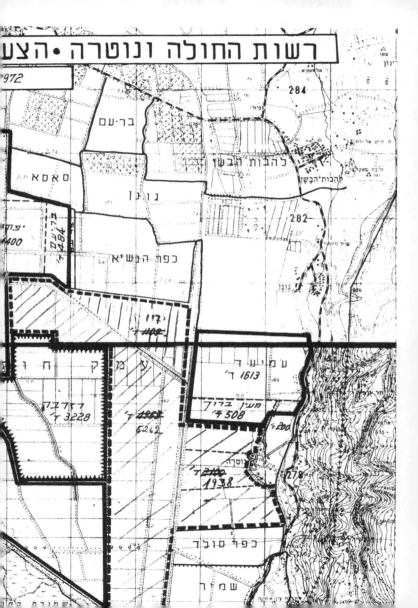

Water in Strife and Action
Simcha Blass, 1973

The tributaries of the Jordan and the springs around Huleh valley that flowed into the river created marshes that swarmed with mosquitoes, making the area a source of blackwater fever. The slopes around the marsh were deeply furrowed, and the water swept the dirt into the valley. The irrigated areas belonged to the effendi in Syria, far away from the fever, and the land was tilled by tenant farmers. The selection law, invalidating family farms on irrigated land, applied here, too. The area of the marsh, called the "concession" and franchised to the effendi in Syria by the Turkish government, was also tilled by tenant farmers at the end of summer, but only at the swamp edge. Two villages, however, Buweiziya and Salihiya, whose fields in the valley were a few meters higher than Jordan level and were not irrigated, were owned by families of felahin.

For many years, attention was turned to the Huleh swamp, until finally "land redeemer" Yehoshua Hankin worked miracles and managed to purchase the concession land, the swamp, ignoring objectors who maintained that the swamp "could wait." The acquisition of the concession, which required the consent of the Mandatory authorities, was also conditioned on draining the swamp and handing part of the dry land to the local cultivators, the tenant farmers. It was clear that with the recovery of the area, land prices would rise in the vicinity of the concession, and the JNF began to concentrate purchases of these lands.

Simcha Blass (1897–1982) was a water engineer, a Zionist activist, and the planner of major water projects for the Jewish settlement in the 1930s and 1940s. His book, *Water in Strife and Action*, is a personal memoir by an engineer and a functionary, and at the same time—an account of Israel's water projects.

* * *

The Palestine Land Development Company (PLDC), on behalf of which Hankin purchased the concession, commissioned a plan for drainage of the swamp and irrigation of the reclaimed land from a well-known English engineering company, Rendel, Palmer and Tritton (RPT report). In its proposal, the firm included—and rightly so—areas bordering the concession, and came up with a plan that suited Egyptian or Indian agriculture. It included half a dozen channels whose mild natural slopes run from north to south, which would have transformed the dry land into a new marsh—but would have necessitated a dictator to divide the water between farmers, introducing yet another complication: intensive farming practiced by Jews versus extensive farms practiced by Arabs—a multifold mixture.

RPT's plan came into my hands, and I could see it was not suitable for us—on top of our reluctance at dependence on a water-distributing dictator, who would probably be English, whereas we adhered to independence. I explained to Eliezer Kaplan (then head of the Settlement Department) and to Avraham Granot (then director-general of the JNF) the faults and shortcomings of the RPT plan, and instead proposed an independent water plan, which was based on a main water carrier along the eastern slope of Huleh, where we have already concentrated a substantial land mass. From this main conduit it would be possible to connect pressure pipes, which could run in a winding route so as not to pass through areas not owned by us and carry the water to our land, but there was a war at the time and nothing was done.

* * *

When the State of Israel was established, the Huleh swamp was shifted to the care of the Ministry of Commerce and

Industry, since the marshland was classified as a "concession," and concessions were handled by that ministry. The concessions administrators were lawyers, who are sometimes indeed capable of pulling a person from a quagmire, but are incapable of draining or irrigating one. As we all know, no one gives up power, even on an issue in which one is not versed. The Minister of Agriculture in the Provisional Government, A. Zisling, however, obtained an agreement from the Minister of Trade and Industry that this concession would be handled by both ministries. A committee was appointed, with two chairmen: myself, as director of the Water Department, and the concession supervisor. The lawyers got out of the swamp, and the Water Department began work on the area's draining and irrigation plan. The Huleh Draining Department was established, headed by engineer A. Kublanov, who had previously planned the draining of Baron Rothschild's Kebarah marshland. The draining plan had a "patron"—JNF—to whom the concession was transferred, and which also owned the adjacent lands. The work was contracted to an American company, which brought in special machinery—drawing soil with water—and despite the Syrian opposition, the work was completed. Lake Huleh disappeared, and the swamp was drained. Nature conservation advocates objected to the drainage due to the extinction of endemic flora and fauna, but they ultimately settled for a 1,000-acre nature reserve.

323

Cutting down the papyrus forest, 1950

326 ‹The Draining Project›

Bulldozers against the backdrop of a bridge over the Jordan river, 1952–53; original caption: "Changing nature in the Huleh area; 'The wilderness and the solitary place shall be glad for them; and the desert shall rejoice, and blossom as the rose' (Isaiah 35:1)" (album: Arie Ilan)

Tractor stuck in a peat field, 1958 (photo: Peter Merom)

The world is a blank slate. The mountain asks to be quarried: you can hear its dull creaking in the depths of the earth, begging for the touch of the axe and tractor, yearning for us to strike it, to cut sections off, to gape it open and lay it bare. The river that flowed here from time immemorial has succumbed to the pump and the pipe. Swamp and lake drain to nothingness.

Last Boat Ride on Lake Huleh
Ephraim Talmi, 1957

Drainage of Lake Huleh was nearing completion, and I knew that a magnificent lake, set in the Huleh Valley between the Golan Heights to the east, Mount Hermon to the north, and the Naphtali Mountains to the west, would disappear in the coming days. I knew that the dam's opening would be the act concluding a series of actions performed over the past five years: draining the Huleh marshes, reclaiming thousands of hectares of fine land that had been flooded with water, quicksand, and wild vegetation, for agricultural cultivation. I wanted to come to Lake Huleh and imprint this wonderful sight, a sight that was being removed from the country's map, in my memory forever. When the draining began, I made a thorough visit to the lake and marshland. We ascended along the Jordan River into the richest jungle we ever had in our country. We reached as far as the northern edge of the Huleh marshland, all the way to the border of Kibbutz Ne'ot Mordechai. I then scorched in my mind the majestic views of a magnificent sanctuary of nature, rich not only in water, but also in rare flora and fauna.

Ephraim Talmi (1905–1982), a writer, translator, and journalist, worked in agriculture during his first years in the country.

We knew that the end had come to an enchanted magical world. We knew that the marshland occupied an area of 6,000 hectares and had to be drained to eliminate the fever, provide bread to thousands of new settlers, and abundant food to the country's population. It is wrong to waste such abundance of water on wild, exploitative vegetation, waging a free-for-all with itself. The Jordan, the Dan, and the Hasbani, as well as other springs that join them, have formed many waterways, and these fed the broad swamps and their lush vegetation, which sustained countless animals. Millions of cubic meters of good water were lost; they either evaporated in the scorching heat, or gulped by the plants. Thousands of hectares of excellent soil were unused. We knew that this kind of situation was unacceptable. At the same time, we regretted this act, which clearly could not be delayed; because we were well aware that with the draining operations, a rare, charming corner of nature would be destroyed.

The great task of draining the swamps and the Huleh has now been completed by the Jewish National Fund (JNF). The Huleh authority already holds approximately 3,000 hectares of land fit for cultivation, and when the dam's gate is lifted, the lake's water will leave its permanent place for generations and there will be no more Lake Huleh or waters of Merom. Who will know in the years to come about the swamps that were once here, and the rich, wonderful kingdom of flora and fauna? Local nature lovers tried to prevent this before it was too late. They wanted to save at least a part of this precious nook from extinction; they endeavored to establish a nature reserve, and reached all the parties dealing with the eradication of the marshes and the lake. It was agreed to leave an area of more than 200 hectares of land in which the animals could continue to live in the thicket unique to the Huleh, where they have lived throughout the years.

332 ‹ The Draining Project ›

Peter Merom was born in November 1919 in Silesia, Germany, and emigrated to Palestine in 1934. In 1938 he settled in Kibbutz Hulata on the shore of Lake Huleh and worked as a fisherman alongside the other kibbutz members. With a pocket camera he purchased in 1935, he began photographing the lake and the fishermen working, and when the Huleh draining project began—he documented it, too. Merom is one of the best known photographers of the local landscape, and his book *The Death of the Lake* (Heb. The Song of a Dying Lake) recorded a world that disappeared from existence.

Photographs and text from Peter Merom's *The Death of the Lake*, 1960 »

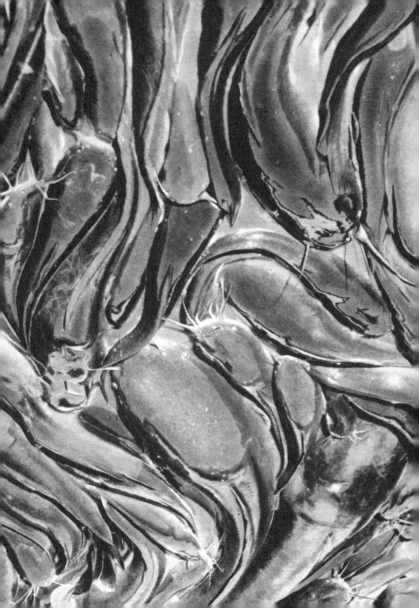

The Death of the Lake
Peter Merom, 1960

But one day the die was cast. Sections of machinery were brought in and assembled, tractors began to nibble at the edges of the swamp. Weeks passed, perhaps months, and suddenly a giant dredging machine gleamed in the sunlight. slowly it floated within the trench it had dug for itself in the heart of the swamp, slowly it dug its teeth into the soil, into mould formed over centuries by the vegetation which renewed itself every summer.

It dug its teeth in and with snail-like pace, step by step, day by day, made its way through the tangle human eyes had never viewed, on which the sun had never shone. The mounds of earth grew, were mixed with water and carried off in pipes. Startled birds left their homes and went forth to seek new ones. Their dwellings were destroyed. Puddles beside the newly-dug trench drained into it, leaving behind them mournful patches of bareness, hinting of what was to come, the unbelievable.

And the trenches grew longer and longer, like the charted lines on the map of the vigilant engineer.

‹ The Draining Project ›

The Huleh draining project began in 1951 and was completed in 1958. Following it, the lake's bed was transformed into agricultural land: it was redefined, divided into agricultural plots, and granted to the area settlements. The Huleh Development Authority was established to coordinate the agricultural transformation of the land: food and cotton crops were selected, seed portions of the selected crop varieties were distributed, mechanical equipment was purchased, and irrigation systems were laid throughout the valley. In propaganda films of the time, the draining is presented as a tremendous achievement of progress: green fields overflowing with crops replace what used to be a swamp infested with malaria mosquitoes, heralding days of plenty. For a moment it seemed like success story.

Swamp transformed into agricultural land (still shots from the film *Hope from the Huleh*, 1950)

Hopes soon gave way to reality, the lake's draining led to an ecological disaster. The project caused the loss of a large body of freshwater, the disappearance of a rich, unique habitat, and a severe damage to the local plant and animal population. Some species whose only place of distribution was Huleh have completely disappeared from the country: the white-tailed eagle (of which some individuals were released into the wild in the 1970s to renew its population in the area), the European water vole, the African darter, and the Huleh painted frog (rediscovered in 2011). In addition, endemic species of fish were extinct: the Huleh bream and Tristramella simonis intermedia. Another endemic fish species, the Oxynoemacheilus galilaeus, was seriously endangered. Additional populations of mammals, birds, and amphibians were harmed as a result of the demolition of the unique habitat, and all those living off or sustained by the lake and the marsh were displaced.

The lake's draining resulted in subsidence and a drop in the aquifer water level. The lake's peat soil, which was supposed to be extremely fertile, turned out to be poor, and its cultivation posed a great many difficulties to farmers. Moreover, it was also discovered that the lake served as an intermediate basin for organic substances carried in the upper Jordan's runoff, and that the swamp served as a filtration and purification system for the water before flowing into the Sea of Galilee. When the basin was drained and the marsh vegetation disappeared, nitrogen compounds were released from the soil and drifted to the Sea of Galilee, causing increased seaweed growth and damage to the fish and the quality of drinking water. Zionism's project of heroic abundance turned out to be an ecological disaster and an agricultural fiasco. The modern dream of a valley of profusion was shattered.

All this also applies to the water buffaloes. Since the beginning of the 20th century, the population of water buffaloes has steadily declined. The females' milk yield was very limited in comparison to that of the Hebrew cows, and their use as beasts of burden has become increasingly redundant in a world of machinery and tractors. Destruction of the Huleh habitat was the last and final stage in their complete disappearance from the local landscape.

At the end of the 1967 War, a small herd of water buffaloes was discovered in the valley of Betiha (descending from the Golan Heights) and brought to the Huleh reserve. Nowadays this small herd lives in a fenced area near the Huleh reservoir.

‹The Draining Project›

Fire in the Valley. The earth was burning as in an apocalyptic vision. Pits of fire gathered underground. Smoke billowed above the split ground, and sandstorms rose and hid the sun's eye.

The drying of peatlands on the lake's bed turned out to be an exothermic heat-emitting process, causing spontaneous subterranean combustions that could sometimes go on for months. The fire pits, four to five meters in diameter, reached the depth of groundwater.

The dry soil lost its organic components and strength, and disintegrated. Blowing winds caused great amounts of dust to rise into the air. The topsoil was swept away. The surface gradually sank.

In the 1990s, in an attempt to raise the level of the aquifer and improve the quality of the Sea of Galilee water, the state flooded a tiny portion of the fields to create a mini-lake (Heb. *agamon*).

In 2007, the "Peat Treaty" was signed. The state agreed to charge low water rates in exchange for farmers' pledge to water and irrigate 3,000 hectares of peat land, even if unsuitable for field crops, to prevent their combustion.

In 1998, the Jewish National Fund transformed the mini-lake into a tourist attraction. Crowds of visitors come to watch the migratory fowl camp on site. To ensure that the birds do not consume all the crops, the nature inspectors provide them with generous portions of corn. The free meals encourage many migratory birds to spend the winter in Israel.

Dry peat fields on fire, 1958–59 (photo: Peter Merom)

Last Thoughts on Plenitude.

In 1951, the year in which the draining project began, Mekorot, Israel's National Water Company, carried out work at 'Ain Mallaha (Ma'ayan Eynan) flowing into Lake Huleh. As part of the work, underground fuel installations were put in place to feed the water pumps, and during the excavations a prehistoric settlement from the Natufian period, dating to 11,700 to 15,000 years ago, was unearthed.

The people who lived by the spring, the lake, and the marsh were hunter-gatherers. It was a sedentary settlement some 4,000 years before the agricultural revolution, where the world's oldest historical evidence of stone house construction and domestication of dogs was found—the first step in the complex relationship between humans and animals, and perhaps more accurately—a step that distinguished humans from animals.

Houses dug some half a meter in the ground were unearthed on site, whose walls were made of stone and their ceiling consisted of a set of rods on which reed mats were spread. Many graves of variously aged men and women were discovered, as well as evidence of widespread worship and elaborate exploitation of nature. Evidence of the usage of wild wheat seeds was found, as well as animal bones cooked in fire, including fallow deer, wild boar, tortoise, and fish. The Huleh's unique environment—with its abundance of freshwater and zoological and botanical wealth—provided the ideal conditions for establishing one of the world's first permanent settlements. Nature's abundance allowed this ancient group of people to settle down, build a home, bury their dead, sanctify them, and tie their fate with that of the animals.

15,000-year old fish hooks made of bone, discovered in the Jordan River Dureijat archeological site in the southern Huleh Valley (photo: Gonen Sharon)

‹ Last Thoughts on Plenitude ›

This young woman was brought to burial; 35 at the time of her death. She was buried in a grave dug in the floor of the house, topped by a large slab of limestone. She was placed in a fetal position on her right side, her left palm under her forehead and her right hand on a puppy's body curled up near the corpse's head. Their special bond is clearly evident even today, 14,500 years after they were buried in a hug. This archaeological finding is the earliest evidence of dog domestication in the world.

This woman was one of the last hunter-gatherers in the area, just before wheat was domesticated and the agricultural revolution that changed the world was set in motion. She lived in a village, in a house which had stone walls for the first time in history. Fishing in the shallow lake waters, hunting crabs and water turtles, as well as deer, fallow deer, and wild boar, and roasting them over the fire, were easy. The world provided them their every need.

Burial of a woman with a dog, Ain Mallaha (Eynan), 14,500 years ago (the Upper Galilee Museum of Prehistory, Kibbutz Ma'ayan Baruch; photo: Gonen Sharon)

Bunker
Epilogue

A solitary asphalt road stretches across a dusty desert.

Air-conditioned, protecting its passengers from the great heat, the car advances along the route descending from the Jerusalem mountains eastward to the territories occupied in 1967. At the end of the road, the Dead Sea can be seen every now and then, as well as plantations of tall palm trees. Forty minutes later, we turn right towards the Qasr el-Yahud baptism site. Some say that it was here that the Israelites crossed the Jordan River on their return from Egypt to the land of Canaan; it was here that Jesus was baptized by John the Baptist; and it is here that worshippers come, dressed in white robes, to soak in the water of the narrow, muddy channel and be sanctified by imitating the deeds of the Lord. The river's route is visible from afar like a wriggling green serpent at the heart of the desert valley. Monasteries and churches are scattered along the way.

Gili Merin, Qasr al-Yahud near Jericho, 2018 »

About 100 meters before the baptism site, the driver turns right, climbs a hill, and stops the car near a large military D9 bulldozer. The IDF is currently busy neutralizing and removing the many mines left in the area, and is preparing the place for pilgrimage tourism in the land of monasteries. We get out of the car in the scorching heat and climb up the hill on sloping ground. At the top of the hill is an abandoned military post, a bunker hidden in a mound. We put on headlights and enter the bowels of the earth.

Steep iron stairs go down and down, followed by a tunnel that stretches a few steps in a straight line and then turns left. We walk in a file inside modular steel corridors. We are in total darkness now, only the headlights' beams faintly illuminate the way, wavering. On occasion we discover a dusty shelf laden with canned food, and four steel bunk bed frames, one in each corner of the subterranean room. There is a strange smell in the air and the echoing sounds of clattering and clicking. As I lift my head toward the ceiling, it moves with dozens of shades of darkness, a wave of mysterious movement. The steel ceiling is padded with bats hanging with their heads down, close together, their wings folded and they lightly sway in the dim light. There is life in the darkness.

Pest Control. Since the 1960s, the Plant Protection unit in the Ministry of Agriculture conducted pest control operations against Egyptian fruit bats that have, in their view, damaged agricultural produce in the fields. (It was later found that the bats usually feed on ripe fruit and do not pose an agricultural threat, since in most plantations fruit is harvested before ripening).

Bats establish their colonies mainly in caves, or in other dark and secluded places such as attics, basements, and underground parking lots. Their disinfestation was carried out by "cave fumigation": Lindane (gammaxene)—a type of nerve gas—is spread in the cave, which is subsequently sealed with a tarpaulin. This results in the rapid eradication of the bat population living in that cave.

During repeated cave fumigation operations, the population of insect-eating microbats—which actually benefit farmers, as they eat pests such as moths, beetles, aphids, and flies, that damage agricultural produce—was severely damaged. 32 species of microbats are known in Israel, and all of them were severely affected by pest control operations, some to the point of total disappearance from the country.

The cave fumigation operations were only stopped in the 1990s. In 2018, it was proposed to include fruit bats in the list of protected species, but the law is yet to be applied to them.

New War against Fruit Robbers
Haaretz, 3.7.1959

The quantity of apricot that reached the markets twenty years ago was far greater than it is today. This fruit, which is grown mainly by Arabs, did not give way to other fruits; growers in many places simply stopped growing it due to the great damage caused by nocturnal fruit robbers—the flying foxes (fruit bats), which, unlike ordinary bats, are not beneficial to man, but rather detrimental. With the expansion of plantations across the country, the damage caused by this nightly pest has increased. In Israel we are dealing with an average-sized bat, its body length reaches about 16 cm and its wing span is close to one meter. In the island of Sumatra there are bats about 40 cm in length and wingspan of approximately 1.5 meters. In these islands, the fruit robber is hunted using nets, and its meat, which tastes like rabbit meat, is eaten.

Bandits by Night
Many localities whose main livelihood depends on fruit trees often complain about the damage caused at night by large colonies of bats. Initially, this pest was fought by repellents and the occasional shot from a carbine cannon, which alarmed the bats. But in doing so, they were merely expelled from one plantation to another, and were not eradicated. In recent years, the bat population has grown dramatically. In the daytime they are not visible, only leaving their hiding places—caves, recesses in the mountains, wells, and deserted warehouses or buildings—about two hours after sunset. Those who do not look for them will not see them, because they hang silently by their feet between roof beams or cracks.

Bats can cover great distances in one night, so there is no doubt that some of the nocturnal thieves come to us for nightly robberies, even from across the border. There is nothing we can do about it. Against tens of thousands or hundreds of thousands of bats residing locally, a war has now been waged in ways unknown to date.

Explosives and Fumigation Agents

Mr. Y. Naftali, one of the veteran employees of the Plant Protection division, discusses his success in destroying bats using explosives and fumigation agents. Last year, a message was received from Mr. Braverman of Yazur near Tel Aviv, informing about a large population of fruit bats in an old well. The field team headed there, blocked the well with plastic sheets, and dropped six lit Lindane flares seven meters deep. [...] When they removed the sheet from the well's mouth, they found 1,200 dead bats inside. After less than six months, bats again gathered in this well, and the operation was repeated.

In another experiment in the Carmel caves, explosives were used to destroy the nocturnal fruit bats, while closing the cave's mouth. Since the Plant Protection Services unit did not want to damage the cave, they sought the help of the Engineering Corps, which used two kg of TNT. This amount was not enough to eliminate the entire bat population, and some managed to escape from the cave mouth. Therefore, it was decided to make a second attempt [...] and this time the entire population of bats was destroyed without damage to the cave. Two months later, a new bat population had arrived, and the method of Lindane flares was tried along with a more complicated closure of the cave with plastic sheeting. Three days later the cave was opened, and 2,500 bat carcasses were found inside.

364 ‹Epilogue›

List of caves inhabited by bats, the Israeli Nature Conservancy, 1970

מדינת ישראל

משרד החקלאות
אזור הגליל–צפת
השלוחה בקרית שמונה
תאריך : 9/3/75
מספר
הגנת הצומח / 429

אל: מר דב ירמיה, הרשות לשמורת הטבע.

הנדון:– עטלפי פירות בוואדי אסל.

ברךתי עם שמחה גלר, הוא היה בוואדי אסל ואיתר את המקום אשר שם נמצאים העטלפים.

סוכם בינינו שהוא יבצע את ההדברה. הבעיה שהוא מוכן לבצע את זה בעוד שבועיים בערך, אבל המצב הוא, שכל לילה יש נזק רב בבית האריזה האיזורי בקרית – שמונה, עשרה ק"ג כל לילה, והנזק הכספי כל לילה הוא גדול.

אני מבקש התחשבות במצב, ולראות את המסימה הזו כדחופה ביותר ולהקדים את הפעולה.

התקבל

בכבוד רב ,
ספר שאול
עוזר לעניני הגנת הצומח.

העתק:–
הנהלת הג.

צפת, רח' הפלמ"ח 1217, טל (067) 30845/6
קרית-שמונה, בנין המועצה האזורית, טל. (067) 40977/8

Correspondence on bat extermination between officials in the Ministry of Agriculture and the Nature Conservancy, 1975

Bat carcasses after cave fumigation, Bitan Aharon, 1980

‹ Epilogue ›

In 1994, a peace agreement was signed between the State of Israel and the Kingdom of Jordan. Following the agreement, the IDF cleared a series of bunkers along the Jordan Valley boundary, between the Dead Sea in the south and the Golan Heights in the north. The border became a mined demilitarized zone, devoid of all traffic, strewn with underground reinforced tunnels.

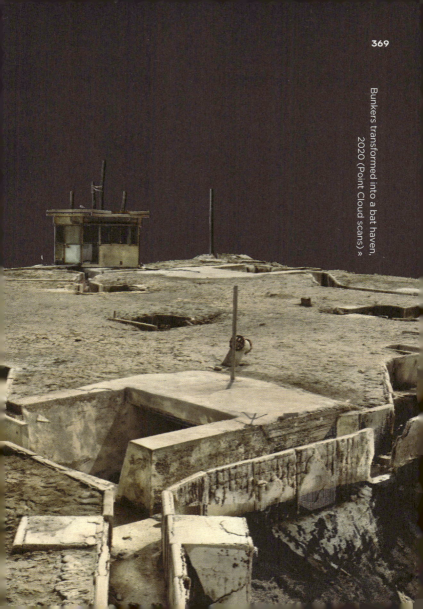

Bunkers transformed into a bat haven, 2020 (Point Cloud scans) »

Geoffroy's Horseshoe bat at Allenby Bridge Military Outpost, 2011 (photo: Eran Levin)

‹ Epilogue ›

In 2007, bat researcher Dr. Eran Levin of Tel Aviv University, and Aviam Atar of the Israel Nature and Parks Authority, discovered that one of the bunkers in the vicinity of Jericho, the one adjacent to the Qasr el-Yahud Baptism site in the Land of Monasteries, became a shelter for microbats, previously believed to have disappeared from the country. Following the discovery, the entire chain of abandoned bunkers was explored, and insect-eating microbats of 12 different species, all endangered, were discovered in all of them, hundreds of thousands in total.

In the heart of the desert, underground, no one interferes with the bats' daytime rest, no one pollutes the subterranean space with light, noise, or movement. It is a paradise in darkness, an isolated island where human rule has no reach, and where these animals can thrive again.

Yehuda Ariel, "New War against Fruit Robbers," *Ha'aretz*, 3 July 1959 [Hebrew] / Philip J. Baldensperger, *The Immovable East: Studies of the People and Customs of Palestine* (Boston: Small, Maynard & Co., 1913), p. 175 / David Ben-Gurion, "Address to the Second Knesset's Opening Session, 1949," in Yosef Weitz, *HaYa'ar Ve'haYiur Be'Yisrael* [Forest and Afforestation in Israel] (Ramat Gan: Masada, 1970), p. 295 [Hebrew] / Simcha Blass, *Mei Merivah u-Ma'as* [Water in Strife and Action] (Ramat Gan: Masada, 1973), pp. 105–106 [Hebrew] / Israel Robert Blum, *The Life of Bees in Israel* (Tel Aviv: Mitzpe, 1943) [Hebrew] / Israel Robert Blum, *Man and the Bee: Beekeeping in Israel* (Tel Aviv: Twersky, 1951), pp. 34, 190–191 [Hebrew] / Bernhard von Breydenbach, *Peregrinatio in terram sanctam* (Mainz, 1486) [Latin] / Burchard of Mt. Sion, *Description of the Holy Land*, trans. Aubrey Stewart (London: Palestine Pilgrims' Text Society, 1897), pp. 99–102 / Isabel Burton, *The Inner Life of Syria, Palestine, and the Holy Land: From My Private Journal* (London: Henry S. King & Co., 1875), vol. II, p. 216 / Grace M. Crowfoot and Louise Baldensperger, *From Cedar to Hyssop: A Study in the Folklore of Plants in Palestine* (London: Sheldon Press, 1932), p. 59 / Abbot Daniel, *Pilgrimage of the Russian Abbot Daniel in the Holy Land, Ca. 1106–1107* (London: Palestine Pilgrims' Text Society, 1897), pp. 66–69 / Shmuel Dayan, *Bi'yemei Hazon u'Matzor* [In Days of Vision and Siege] (Tel Aviv: Masada and the Moshavim Movement, 1953), p. 230 [Hebrew] / Itzhak Elazari-Volcani, *The Dairy Industry as a Basis for Colonisation in Palestine* (Tel Aviv: Palestine Economic Society, 1928) / Isaac Elazari-Volcani, *Local Agriculture will be Established* (Rehovot: Agriculture Research Station, 1937), p. 5 [Hebrew] / Moshe Gershoni, "Paddling in the Huleh," *MiBifnim: Organ of the United Kibbutz Movement* (November 1954), pp. 69–83 [Hebrew] / Sir John Hope Simpson, *Palestine: Report on Immigration, Land Settlement and Development*, presented by the Secretary of State for the Colonies to Parliament by Command of his Majesty, October 1930 (London: H.M. Stationery Office, 1930), vol. I, pp. 12–20 / Zvi Ilan, "Black Goats Annihilate without being Eliminated," *Davar*, 12 August 1974 [Hebrew] / S. Layish, "Goats and Fire: The Chief Agents of Damage to the Israeli Forest," *Herut*, 31 March 1959 [Hebrew] / Uriel Levy, *History of Dairy Farming in Israel* (Tel Aviv: The Israeli Cattle Breeders Association, 1983), p. 109 [Hebrew] / John MacGregor, *The Rob Roy on the Jordan, Nile, Red Sea, and Gennesareth: A Canoe Cruise in Palestine and Egypt, and the Waters of Damascus* (London: John Murray, 1869), pp. 286–297 / Henry Maundrell, *A Journey from Aleppo to Jerusalem at Easter, A.D. 1697* (Edinburgh: John Orphoot, 1812), pp. 108–110 / William McClure Thomson, *The Land and the Book, or Biblical Illustrations Drawn from the Manners and Customs, the Scenes and Scenery of the Holy Land* (New York: Harper & Brothers, 1854/1873), vol. I, p. 384 / Peter Merom, *The Death of the Lake* (Tel Aviv: Davar, 1960) [Hebrew] / Shams al-Din al-Muqaddasi, *The Best Divisions for Knowledge of the Regions*, trans. Basil A. Collins (Reading,

UK: Garnet, 2000), pp. 137, 156 / Salman Natour, *Memory Talked to Me and Walked Away* (Tel Aviv: Resling, 2014), p. 45 [Hebrew] / Ami Neria, *Veterinary Medicine in Eretz-Israel: Fifty Years of Veterinary Medicine, 1917–1967* (Tel Aviv, 2001), pp. 12–15 [Hebrew] / Tamar Novick, *Milk & Honey: Technologies of Plenty in the Making of a Holy Land, 1880–1960* (Ph.D. dissertation, Department of History and Sociology of Science, University of Pennsylvania, 2014) / Tamar Novick, "All about Stavit: A Bovine Biography," *Theory and Criticism*, 51 (Winter 2019), pp. 15–40 [Hebrew] / Paula of Rome, in Molly Hand (ed.), *Women's Writings on Christian Spirituality* (New York: Dover, 2013), p. 9 / The Piacenza Pilgrim, *Of the Holy Places Visited by Antoninus Martyr*, trans. Aubrey Stewart (Palestine Pilgrims' Text Society, 1884), p. 5 / George Pitt, "Palestine," *The British Friend*, 40:33 (1882), pp. 257–258 / Isaiah Press, *Eretz Israel and Southern Syria: Travel Book* (Jerusalem, Berlin & Vienna: Benjamin Harz, 1921), pp. 41–45 [Hebrew] / R. (member of the Labor and Defense Battalion in Migdal), "On the Shores of the Sea of Galilee," *HaSolel*, 29 January 1921, pp. 77–78 [Hebrew]; translation quoted from: Boaz Neumann, *Land and Desire in Early Zionism*, trans. Haim Watzman (Waltham, MA: Brandeis University Press, 2011), pp. 110–111 / R. Moshe Reicher, *Schare Jerusalem* [The Gates of Jerusalem] (Lemberg: Nik, 1867/1870), p. 31 [Hebrew] / Rendel, Palmer and Tritton, "Huleh Basin: Report, Preliminary Scheme and Estimates for Reclamation of the Huleh Lake and Marshes and Drainage and Irrigation in the Basin," July 1936, pp. 10–11; State Archives, ISA-MandatoryOrganizations-pubBritishMandate-001n4c7 / David Sadeh and Zvi Palgi, interviewed by Rachel Shai, *The Beekeeper from Gan Shmuel: In Memory of David Reicher Ardi* (Kibbutz Gan Shmuel, 1987) [Hebrew] / Shalom Scherer, *Zoometry* (Tel Aviv: Michlol, 1976), pp. 5–14, 22–39, 50–52 [Hebrew] / David Schub, "Memoirs," in Abraham Ya'ari (ed.), *The Goodly Heritage: Memoirs Describing the Life of the Jewish Community of Eretz-Yisrael from the Seventeenth to the Twentieth Centuries* (Jerusalem: The Zionist Organization, 1947), vol. 1, chap. 47, p. 535 [Hebrew] / Ami Shamir, "100,000 Litters from one udder! Interview with Stavit from Kfar Giladi and Her Grooms," *Bamahane*, 27 July 1950 [Hebrew] / Abraham Shlonsky, "Here" and "Produce," in *Writings: Poems*, vol. II (Tel Aviv: Sifriyat Poalim, 1971) [Hebrew]; English version: Itamar Gov / Ephraim Talmi, "Last Boat Ride on Lake Huleh," *Davar*, 10 November 1957 [Hebrew] / Henry Baker Tristram, "The Fauna and Flora of Palestine," in *The Survey of Western Palestine* (Jerusalem: BEF, 1884) / Henry Baker Tristram, *The Land of Israel: A Journal of Travels in Palestine, Undertaken with Special Reference to its Physical Character, 1863–1864* (London: Society for Promoting Christian Knowledge, 1865), pp. 85–87, 411–412, 447 / Meyer Weisgal (ed.), *Palestine Book: Official Publication of the Jewish Palestine Pavilion at the New York World's Fair 1939* (New York: Pavilion Publications, 1939) / Yosef Weitz, "August 17, 1941," *My Diary and Letters to the Children*, vol. 2: *Posts and*

Bibliography

Outposts (Tel Aviv: Masada, 1965), p. 187 [Hebrew] / Yosef Weitz, *HaYa'ar Ve'haYiur Be'Israel* [Forest and Afforestation in Israel] (Ramat Gan: Masada, 1970), p. 513 [Hebrew] / John Wilkinson, "Hugeburc's Life of Willibald" [ca. 780], in Wilkinson, *Jerusalem Pilgrims Before the Crusades* (Warminster: Aris & Phillips, 1977), p. 128 / Yehuda Ya'ari, *Like Glittering Light: A Novel* (Jerusalem: Association of Hebrew Writers in Jerusalem/Ogdan, 1937), p. 208 [Hebrew]; translation quoted from: Boaz Neumann, *Land and Desire in Early Zionism*, trans. Haim Watzman (Waltham, MA: Brandeis University Press, 2011), p. 86 / Yehuda Ya'ari, *When the Candle was Burning*, trans. Menahem Hurwitz (London: Victor Gollancz, 1946) / Emmanuel Yalan, *The Moshav Farm* (Tel Aviv: Israel Ministry of Agriculture, 1959), p. 7 [Hebrew] / Michael Zohary and Naomi Feinbrun-Dothan, drawn by Ruth Koppel, *Flora Palaestina* (Tel Aviv: Israel Academy of Sciences and Humanities, 1966) / "Palestine Honey Production," report by the U.S. Consul in Jerusalem, 2 November 1921; USNA/US State Department, Records Relating to the Internal Affairs of Turkey, 1910–1929; film reel 86 / Press release by the British Mandate Government, 25 July 1933, the Central Zionist Archives, CZA/S90/2121/1 / "The Arab, The Goat and the Camel: Destroyers of the Desert," *The Palestine Post*, 11 October 1934 / "Plant Protection (Damage by Goats) Law, 1950," in *Laws of the State of Israel*, vol. 4, 5710–1949/50, trans. the Ministry of Justice (Israel: the Government Printer, 1950), pp. 181–182 / "Bat Extermination Operation", *She'arim*, 31 January 1960 [Hebrew] / "The Black Goat Endangers the Galilee Forests," *Haaretz*, 22 December 1960 [Hebrew] / "Letter to the Editor," *The Jerusalem Post*, 15 June 1978 (translated from the Hebrew version) / Plant Protection (Damage by Goats, Cancellation) Law, 2018; Israeli Knesset Legislative Record Series, in *Hatza'ot Chok HaKnesset* no. 759, 12 February, 2018, p. 96 [Hebrew] / Protocol of Knesset Session of 7 May 2018: Plant Protection Bill (Damage by Goats, Cancellation), 2018, second and third readings.

‹ Index of Images and Sources ›

The archival materials in this catalogue—photographs, images, texts, etc.—have been obtained courtesy of the copyright holders, archives, institutions, and individuals listed below:

Abbreviations: ABB—Armbruster's Bildersammlung zur Bienenkunde (Ludwig Armbruster's Apiary Photo Collection), on permanent loan from the University of Hohenheim to the Domäne Dahlem, Germany / **AE**—Avital Efrat / **BBPC**—Bouky Boaz Collection of Israeli Photography / **BPC**—Nadav Mann, Bitmuna / **CCG**—The Center for Computational Geography, Department of Geography, the Hebrew University of Jerusalem / **CZA**—Central Zionist Archives / **DCBA**—Dairy Cattle Breeders Association / **EES**—Estate of Ephraim Shmaragd, Nir Mann Collection / **GPO**—Israel Government Press Office / **GSE**—The Gretel Saalheimer Estate / **HHA**—HaShomer HaTzair Archives at Yad Yaari Research and Documentation Center / **HJP**—Historical Jewish Press archives, National Library of Israel and Tel Aviv University / **HMA**—The Heinrich Mendelssohn Archives, Tel Aviv University / **ISA**—Israel State Archives / **KA**—Israeli Knesset Archives / **KCH**—The Knesset Channel / **KGA**—Kibbutz Kfar Giladi Archives / **KKL**—Jewish National Fund (KKL-JNF) Photo Archive / **KTA**—Kiryat Tivon Historical Archive / **MDF**—Dr. Sivan Lacker and Arch. David Lacker, Mutual Dairy Farming / **NLI**—Eran Laor Cartographic Collection, National Library of Israel / **SJFA**—The Steven Spielberg Jewish Film Archive, the Hebrew University of Jerusalem / **USNA**—United States National Archives / **YA**—Yossi Ardi / **YBZ**—Yad Izhak Ben-Zvi / **YSNL**—The Younes and Soraya Nazarian Library, University of Haifa / **ZE**—Zvi Efrat / **ZS**—Zvi Singer

pp. 50–59: pages from John Hope Simpson, *Palestine: Report on Immigration, Land Settlement and Development* (London: H.M. Stationery Office, 1930) / pp. 62, 65: illustrations from Charles William Wilson (ed.), *Picturesque Palestine, Sinai, and Egypt* (Boston, MA: D. Appleton & Co., 1881–84) / pp. 69–73: Bernhard von Breydenbach, *Map of the Holy Land,* 1486; NLI / pp. 67–73: illustrations by Erhard Reuwich, from Bernhard von Breydenbach, *Peregrinatio in terram sanctam* (Mainz, 1486) / pp. 75–83: pages from Henry Baker Tristram, *The Survey of Western Palestine* (London: The Committee of the Palestine Exploration Fund, 1884) / p. 93: aerial photos by Zoltan Kluger, from Meyer Weisgal (ed.), *Palestine Book: Official Publication of the Jewish Palestine Pavilion at the New York World's Fair 1939* (New York: Pavilion Publications, 1939) / pp. 94–97: pages from Weisgal (ed.), *ibid* / p. 115: Curved route designed for reducing bovine stress en-route to the milking parlor (design: Dr. Sivan Lacker, arch.: David Lacker); MDF / pp. 116–117, 137: photographer unknown; image from Ami Shamir, "100,000 Liters from One Udder! Interview with Stavit from Kfar Giladi and her Grooms," *Bamahane*, 27 July 1950 [Hebrew]; KGA / pp. 118–120: images from Ami

386 ‹Index of Images and Sources›

Neria, ***Veterinary Medicine in Eretz-Israel: Fifty Years of Veterinary Medicine, 1917-1967*** (Tel Aviv, 2001) / p. 121: photo by Yaacov Katznelson, 1930; BPC / p. 123: photographer unknown, ca. 1925; YBZ / p. 125: title page of I. Elazari-Volcani, ***The Dairy Industry as a Basis for Colonisation of Palestine*** (Tel Aviv: Palestine Economic Society, 1928) / p. 126: photos by Zoltan Kluger, 1941 (above), 1936 (below); ISA / p. 127: photos by Naftali Oppenheim, ca. 1930; ISA / p. 128: photo by Zoltan Kluger, 1936; ISA / p. 129: photo by Israel Golan (Paikale), 1915; BPC / pp. 130-131: photographer unknown, 1930s; BPC / p. 133: photo by Zvi (Maki) Marcus, 1981; DCBA / p. 134: photographer unknown, 1946; EES / pp. 136-151: images from the Stavit Collection; KGA / pp. 152-153: photographer unknown; the Arvin Yacobi Negative Prints Collection, CZA / p. 155: photographer unknown, 1920s; ZE / pp. 158-159: Architect Richard Kauffmann, 1921; CZA / pp. 160-161: photo by Zoltan Kluger, 1938; ISA / pp. 162-163: model photo from Emmanuel Yalan, ***New Moshav Farmyard*** (Tel Aviv: Israel Ministry of Agriculture, 1959) [Hebrew] / pp. 164-169: zoometric drawings from Shalom Scherer, ***Zoometry*** (Tel Aviv: Michlol, 1976) [Hebrew] / pp. 170-171: United Kibbutz Planning Department, 1985; CZA / pp. 186-187: photo by Azaria Alon, 1960s; AE / p. 189: USNA / p. 192: illustration by Israel Robert Blum, ***The Life of Bees in Israel*** (Tel Aviv: Mitzpe, 1943) [Hebrew] / p. 193: photo from Leonhard Bauer, ***Volksleben im lande der Bibel*** (Leipzig: H.G. Wallmann, 1903) / pp. 194-195: photo by Ludwig Armbruster, ca. 1890; ABB / p. 197: photographer unknown, 1928; YA / p. 198: photographer unknown, ca. 1890; ABB / pp. 200-202: photos by Ludwig Armbruster, 1890; ABB / p. 206: photographer and date unknown; courtesy of Roni Kenigsberg and Kibbutz Yagur Archives, YSNL / p. 207: photo by Zoltan Kluger, 1937; ISA / pp. 208-209: drawings from Israel Robert Blum, ***The Life of Bees in Israel*** (Tel Aviv: Mitzpe, 1943); and ***Man and the Bee: Beekeeping in Israel*** (Tel Aviv: Twersky, 1951) [Hebrew] / pp. 210-211: photo by Azaria Alon, 1960s; AE / pp. 213-215: photographer unknown, 1936; YA / pp. 216-217: photo by Sarale Gur Lavi, 2019 / pp. 218-219, 233: photo from Dov Becker, ***Sheep and Goat Rearing*** (Ein Harod: Hebrew Shepherds Association, 1948) [Hebrew]; Sheep Breeders Collection, HHA / pp. 220-221: photo from the Mitzpe Album; Herbert and Edwin Samuel Photo Collection, ISA / pp. 222-223: photo by Zoltan Kluger, 1936; GPO / p. 225: photo by Zoltan Kluger, 1938; ISA / pp. 227-229: photos by Zvi Oron (Oroshkess), 1934; CZA / p. 232: photo from Moshe Schorr, ***The House Goat*** (Tel Aviv: Supervisor of Agricultural Studies, Ministry of Education and Culture, 1949) [Hebrew] / pp. 235-238: Plant Protection Law, 1950; Israeli Knesset Legislative Record Series, KA / p. 239: photo by Beno Rothenberg, 1948; ISA / p. 240: from a petition by Sakhnin village goat owners to the government of Israel, 1952; ISA / p. 241: from a letter by T. Kotzer, Director of the Arab Village Section, to A. Ber-David, General Secretary of the Ministry of Agriculture, 23 November 1950; ISA [Hebrew] / p. 243: photo by Zoltan Kluger, 1946; CZA /

pp. 244-245: photos from Yosef Weitz, **Forest and Afforestation in Israel** (Ramat Gan: Massada, 1970) [Hebrew] / p. 247: from **Maariv**, 6 June 1974, [Hebrew]; HJP / p. 249: photo by Zvi Singer, 2010; ZS / pp. 254-255: protocol of Knesset Session, 7 May 2018; the Knesset Plenary Records, KA / p. 256: Plant Protection (Damage by Goats, Cancellation) Law, 2018; Israeli Knesset Legislative Record Series, KA / p. 257: from a video of the Knesset session, 7 May 2018; KCH / pp. 261-262: photo by Lasar Dunner, 1944; CZA / p. 263: photo by Yaacov Ben-Dov, 1923; KKL / pp. 264-265: photographer unknown, 1935; KKL / p. 267: photographer and date unknown; CZA / p. 268: illustrations from William M. Thomson, **The Land and the Book** (New York: Harper & Brothers, 1854/1873) / pp. 270-271: photos by Zoltan Kluger, 1940, ISA; 1946, GPO / pp. 272-275: aerial photos, 1945, collage: Bar Mussan Levi; CCG / pp. 276-277: aerial photo by Zoltan Kluger, 1938; YSNL / p. 279: photographer unknown, 1951; CZA / pp. 280-281: photo by Peter Merom, ca. 1960; BBPC / pp. 282-297: pages from John MacGregor, **The Rob Roy on the Jordan, Nile, Red Sea, and Gennesareth: A Canoe Cruise in Palestine and Egypt, and the Waters of Damascus** (London: John Murray, 1869) / p. 299: photo from Peter Merom, **The Death of the Lake** (Tel Aviv: Davar, 1961); reproduced courtesy of BBPC / pp. 300-305: drawings from Michael Zohary and Naomi Feinbrun-Dothan, drawn by Ruth Koppel, **Flora Palaestina** (Tel Aviv: Israel Academy of Sciences and Humanities, 1966) / p. 306: photographer unknown, 1935; GSE / p. 307: photo by Zvi Oron (Oroshkess), 1934; CZA / p. 308: photographer unknown, 1935; courtesy of the Hefetz Family, Kinneret, BPC & YSNL / p. 309: photographer and date unknown; Shimon Bekin Album at the Israel Made Visible Digitation Initiative, KTA / pp. 312-319: CZA / p. 323: photographer unknown, ca. 1950; the Zev Vilnay Collection, YBZ (above); 1951, CZA (below) / pp. 324-325: photo by Zoltan Kluger, 1950; GPO / p. 326: photographers unknown, 1951; CZA / p. 327: photo by Zoltan Kluger, 1952-53; Arieh Ilan Album, YBZ / pp. 328-329: photo by Peter Merom, 1958; BBPC / pp. 333-341: images and text from Peter Merom, **The Death of the Lake** (Tel Aviv: Davar, 1961); reproduced courtesy of BBPC / pp. 342-343: film stills from: **Hope from the Huleh**, 1950, photographed and produced by Lasar Dunner for the Jewish National Fund; SJFA / p. 347: photo by Peter Merom, 1958-59; BBPC / pp. 349, 351: photos by Gonen Sharon, 2020 / pp. 364-365: ISA / pp. 366-367: photographer unknown, 1980; HMA / pp. 368-377: scans: Point Cloud / pp. 378-379: photos by Eran Levin, 2009 / p. 392: photo by Zoltan Kluger, 1940; ISA.

Acknowledgments

Thanks

Agricultural Research Organization ARO, Volcani Center: Victoria Soroker; AlefBet Planners: Ronen Feigenbaum, Arch. Vittorio Corinaldi; Archives for the History of Tel Aviv University: Ella Meirson; Bezalel Academy of Arts and Design, Jerusalem: Zohar Gotesman, Pinchas Green, Guy Markovitch, David Zangiri; Resling Publishing House: Idan Zivoni; The Center for Computational Geography, Department of Geography, The Hebrew University of Jerusalem: Adi Ben Nun, Guy Keren, Prof. Daniel Felsenstein; Central Zionist Archives: Anat Banin, Guy Jamo, Yigal Sitry; Centre de recherche français à Jérusalem (CRFJ): Lyse Baer Zerbit; Domäne Dahlem Archive, Berlin: Sabine Danckwerts, Simon Renkert; The Ecological Greenhouse, Kibbutz Ein Shemer: Avital Geva; Hof HaSharon Dairy Farm: Shachar Goodman; The Israel Museum, Jerusalem: Noam Gal, Ahiad Ovadia; Israel Nature and Parks Authority: Guy Sali, Amit Dolev; Kibbutz Hulata Archives: Grazia Ferrazzini; Kibbutz Kfar Giladi Archives: Daniela Ashkenazi; Kibbutz Yad Mordechai Apiary: Pavel Feoktistov; Kiryat Tivon Archive: Shifra Leshem; Liebling Haus, Tel Aviv: Shira Levy Benyemini; Lin's Farm: Youval Lin; The National Library of Israel: Ayelet Rubin; Ramat Hanadiv Nature Park: Tzach Glasser; Refet HaEmek, Kibbutz Yifat: Omri Goldhor; The Steinhardt Museum of Natural History: Dr. Amos Belmaker, Dr. Revital Ben-David-Zaslow, Prof. Tamar Dayan, Dr. Achik Dorchin, Igor Gavrilov, Adi Katz Shapira, Dr. Eran Levin, Erez Maza, Alon Sapan, Dr. Stanislav Volynchik; Tel Aviv-Jaffa Municipality: Jeremie Hoffmann, Miriam Posner, Giyora Yahalom; WaterVive: Yael Ben-Zvi, Alon Mann; Werner Braun Estate: Yehuda Braun, Neatai Braun; Yad Izhak Ben-Zvi Photo Archives: Nir Ortal; Yad Yaari Research and Documentation Center, Givat Haviva: David Amitai, Yonat Rotbain, Michal Schreiber; Yarqon River Authority: David Pargament / Adi Assif, Ronen Bergman, Bouky Boaz, Avital Efrat, Erez Ella, Maayan First, Matan Gal, Yehoshua Gutman, Shay Giat, Dan Handel, Ofri Ilany, Mirav Katri, Ziv Leibu, Nir Mann, Yonatan Mendel, Ph.D., Stav Meron, Falestin Naili, Inas Natour, Miras Natour, Moshe Pe'er, Iris Rywkind Ben-Zour, Oren Sagiv, Michael Sfard, Asaf Shariv, Prof. Yehouda Shenhav-Shahrabani, Noga Shlomi, Dotan Shraiber, Nirit Shraiber, Yossi Slabezki, Yehuda Sprecher, Yuli Tamir, Alona Vinograd, Shira Wilkof, Noa Yafe, Zvi Yemini, Shachar Zur, Hillit Zwick

Special Thanks
Yossi Ardi, Hagit Ben-Yaakov, Mia Bengel, Liat Brix Etgar, Zvi Efrat, Shlomit Ezron Yarkoni, Edna Fast, Ifat Finkelman, NaAma Ginat-Strum, Ali Halabi, Alma Kishon, Meira Kowalsky, Yossi Leshem, Yechiel Menuchin, Ruth Patir, Deborah Pinto Fdeda, Charles and Janine Pulman, Baruch Spiegel, Ora Stibbe, Els Verbakel, Roy Yellin

Last but not least—we wish to thank our families
Ilil Mataish, Liya and Maya Ginat, Lee Zucker-Cohen, Mira and Uria Cohen, Noam and Julie Boker, Bashir and Amir Baransi

Israel Ministry of Culture and Sports
Chili Tropper, Minister of Culture and Sports
Raz Frohlich, General Director
Galit Wahaba Shasho, Director of Culture
Shirit Keessen, Director of Museums and Visual Arts Department
Ronit Aflalo, Director of Budget and Planning
Elena Lulko, Budget and Planning Coordinator

Israel Ministry of Foreign Affairs
Ziv Nevo Kulman, Head of the Cultural Diplomacy Bureau
Anat Gilead, Director of the Arts Department
Yossi Balt, Head of the Visual Arts Unit
Meira Sagy, Director of the Management and Budget Department

Embassy of Israel in Italy
Dror Eydar, Ambassador
Maya Katzir, Cultural Attaché
Eitan Avraham, Consul

Yigal Amedi, Chairman of the Israeli Council of Culture and Art
Judith Gueta, Chairman of the Visual Art Section

Steering Committee
Dr. Arch. Fatina Abreek-Zubiedat, Prof. Arch. Tal Alon Moses,
Arch. Rivka Gutman, Arch. Daniel Mintz, Prof. Arch. Irit Zoref Netanyahu

With the generous support of
Mifal Hapais Lottery Council for Culture and Art; Anatta; Ronny Douek;
Liebling Haus—The White City Center, Tel Aviv; The Department of
Architecture, Bezalel Academy of Arts and Design, Jerusalem; Centre
de recherche français à Jérusalem (CRFJ)

Chickens at the Mikve Israel Agricultural School, 1940 (photo: Zoltan Kluger)